Briefly:
Kant's *Critique of Practical Reason*

The SCM Briefly series

Anselm's *Proslogion* (with the Replies of Gaunilo and Anselm)
Aquinas' *Summa Theologica Part 1* (God, Part I)
Aquinas' *Summa Theologica Part 2* (God, Part II)
Aristotle's *The Nicomachean Ethics*
Ayer's *Language, Truth and Logic*
Bentham's *An Introduction to the Principles of Morals and Legislation*
Descartes' *Meditations on First Philosophy*
Fletcher's *Situation Ethics: The New Morality*
Hume's *Dialogues Concerning Natural Religion*
Hume's *An Enquiry Concerning Human Understanding*
Kant's *Critique of Practical Reason (The Concept of the Highest Good and the Postulates of the Practical Reason)*
Kant's *Groundwork of the Metaphysics of Morals*
Kant's *Religion within the Boundaries of Mere Reason*
Kierkegaard's *Fear and Trembling*
Mill's *On Liberty*
Mill's *Utilitarianism*
Moore's *Principia Ethica*
Nietzsche's *Beyond Good and Evil*
Plato's *The Republic*
Russell's *The Problems of Philosophy*
Sartre's *Existentialism and Humanism*

Briefly: 25 Great Philosophers from Plato to Sartre

Other Books by David Mills Daniel published by SCM Press:

SCM AS/A2 Ethics and Moral Philosophy
SCM Revision Guide: AS/A2 Ethics and Religious Ethics
SCM Revision Guide: AS/A2 Philosophy of Religion

Briefly: Kant's
Critique of Practical Reason (The Concept of the Highest Good and the Postulates of the Practical Reason)

David Mills Daniel

scm press

© David Mills Daniel 2009

Published in 2009 by SCM Press
Editorial office
13–17 Long Lane,
London, ECIA 9PN, UK

SCM Press is an imprint of Hymns Ancient and Modern Ltd
(a registered charity)
St Mary's Works, St Mary's Plain,
Norwich, NR3 3BH, UK
www.scm-canterburypress.co.uk

The author and publisher acknowledge material reproduced from
Immanuel Kant, *Critique of Practical Reason*, translated by W.S.
Pluhar, Indianapolis/Cambridge: Hackett Publishing Company,
2002.
All rights reserved.

British Library Cataloguing in Publication data

A catalogue record for this book is available
from the British Library

978 0 334 04175 7

Typeset by Regent Typesetting, London
Printed and bound by
Bookmarque, Croydon, Surrey

Contents

Introduction

The SCM *Briefly* series is designed to enable students and general readers to acquire knowledge and understanding of key texts in philosophy, philosophy of religion, theology and ethics. While the series will be especially helpful to those following university and A-level courses in philosophy, ethics and religious studies, it will in fact be of interest to anyone looking for a short guide to the ideas of a particular philosopher or theologian.

Each book in the series takes a piece of work by one philosopher and provides a summary of the original text, which adheres closely to it, and contains direct quotations from it, thus enabling the reader to follow each development in the philosopher's argument(s). Throughout the summary, there are page references to the original philosophical writing, so that the reader has ready access to the primary text. In the Introduction to each book, you will find details of the edition of the philosophical work referred to.

In *Briefly: Kant's Critique of Practical Reason (The Concept of the Highest Good and the Postulates of the Practical Reason)*, we refer to Immanuel Kant, *Critique of Practical Reason*, translated by W. S. Pluhar, Indianapolis/Cambridge: Hackett Publishing Company, 2002.

Each *Briefly* begins with an Introduction, followed by a chapter on the Context in which the work was written. Who was this writer? Why was this book written? With Some Key Quotations and some Suggestions for Further Reading, this *Briefly* aims to get anyone started in their philosophical investigation. The Detailed Summary of the philosophical work is followed by a concise chapter-by-chapter Overview and an extensive Glossary and Index of terms.

Bold type is used in the Detailed Summary and Overview sections to indicate the first occurrence of words and phrases that appear in the Glossary. The Glossary also contains terms used elsewhere in this *Briefly* guide and other terms that readers may encounter in their study of Kant's *Critique of Practical Reason (The Concept of the Highest Good and the Postulates of the Practical Reason)*.

The focus of this *Briefly* is on the part of the book dealing with the concept of the highest good and the postulates of the practical reason, which are relevant to the study of the Philosophy of Religion and Ethics/Religious Ethics Units in AS/A2 Religious Studies.

Context

Who was Immanuel Kant?

Immanuel Kant was born in Königsberg, East Prussia, in 1724. Although he did not come from a wealthy background (his father was a saddler), he was able to enrol at the University of Königsberg in 1740, where he showed an interest in science and astronomy as well as philosophy. After graduating, Kant worked as a tutor for a number of years, before returning to Königsberg, as a private lecturer at the university, in 1755. He was appointed professor of logic and metaphysics in 1770.

In many ways, Kant's life is exactly what we would expect that of a professional philosopher to be. In addition to his teaching responsibilities at the university, where his lectures covered such subjects as physics, geography and anthropology, he devoted himself almost entirely to study, thought and writing. In order to use his time efficiently, he rose before five o'clock in the morning, and followed a strict daily routine, allocating fixed periods of time to each activity. However, despite the pressures on time, imposed by his work and his enormous literary output in the latter part of his life, he was not reclusive, enjoying the company of others and conversation.

Kant's unremarkable and modest career and lifestyle are in marked contrast to the impact of his philosophical views, which have profoundly and permanently influenced thinking about metaphysics, moral philosophy and the philosophy of religion. Due to his unorthodox religious views, some of his ideas were also controversial when they were published. In 1794, the government of the religiously conservative King Frederick William II of Prussia, in response to Kant's *Religion Within the Boundaries of Mere Reason*, which questioned aspects of biblical teaching, Christian theology and church organization, instructed him not to write about religion. Kant felt bound to comply with this order until Frederick William's death in 1797. Kant was also an opponent of war and militarism, and an advocate of peaceful methods of resolving international issues.

As well as the *Critique of Practical Reason* (1788), part of which is summarized in this *Briefly*, Kant's books include: *Critique of Pure Reason* (1781; second edition, 1787), *Prolegomena to any Future Metaphysic* (1783), *Groundwork of the Metaphysics of Morals* (1785), *Critique of Judgement* (1790), *Religion within the Boundaries of Mere Reason* (1793), *On Perpetual Peace* (1795) and *Metaphysics of Morals* (1797). Kant died in 1804.

What is the *Critique of Practical Reason*?

The practical reason and its postulates

Kant's *Critique of Practical Reason* is concerned with the practical reason – reason when it is considering matters of morality and applying moral principles – and its operation. In the part of the *Critique of Practical Reason* covered in this *Briefly*, Kant argues that there are certain things, which the practical reason needs to postulate or assume, in order to make complete sense of morality, which, as part of the concept of the highest good for rational beings, includes their receiving happiness in proportion to their moral virtue. These so-called 'postulates of the practical reason' are freedom, immortality of the soul and God.

Freedom and the moral law

Kant has already emphasized the importance of freedom to morality. In the *Groundwork of the Metaphysics of Morals* (*Groundwork*), he argues that the principles of the moral law (see Glossary and below), which are binding unconditionally on all rational beings, including human beings, are not to be found in human nature, or in any part of our ordinary experience, but are discovered *a priori* (that which comes before/is not based on experience: see Glossary and below), through our reason. In order to have wills which are our own, and to be able to adopt maxims or rules of conduct, which comply with the categorical imperative (see Glossary) of the moral law, and to be responsible for our actions, human beings must be free.

But, why do we need God and immortality?

We can see why freedom is so important to morality. But, why do we need God and immortality? It seems particularly strange, in view of the fact that, in the *Groundwork*, Kant lays such stress on the independence of morality and the vital importance of excluding any extraneous elements from moral decision-making. What Kant calls 'heteronomy of the will' arises if people allow their wills to be determined by considerations other than the fitness of their rules of conduct to serve as universal moral laws for all rational beings. The obvious sources of spurious moral principles are such empirical factors as human desires and inclinations. However, heteronomy of the will would also arise if moral principles were taken from an all-perfect divine will. Kant's point is that the autonomy of morality means that actions are not right just because they satisfy certain human desires, maximize happiness or even because they reflect the will of God.

However, although the supreme good for all rational beings is to obey the moral law for its own sake, and thus to be worthy of happiness, human beings' concept of the highest good also includes the notion of the complete good, where they actually receive happiness in proportion to their moral virtue. Kant argues that the practical reason needs to postulate God as the means of ensuring that human beings receive the happiness they deserve. It also needs to postulate immortality, so that they will have the opportunity to become worthy of happiness, through developing a will, which does not need to be commanded, in order to obey the moral law.

Knowledge through morality

For the purposes of morality, therefore, reason, in its practical use, is able to provide what reason, in its theoretical or speculative use, cannot achieve: some knowledge of God and suprasensible reality. In the *Critique of Pure Reason*, Kant maintains that there are strict limits on our theoretical knowledge of the world. He rejects empiricism, which holds that all our knowledge comes from experience, and argues that we structure our sense experience, by imposing upon it what he calls the *a priori* intuitions of time and space. Sense experience is then thought about by means of *a priori* categories of the understanding, such as causality, reality and necessity. Thus, so far from originating in experience, the *a priori* intuitions and categories originate in human beings themselves, and are part of the way we experience the world. Therefore, no legitimate inference can be made from them to what the world is like in itself. However, Kant also rejects the rationalist view that human beings have a faculty of intellectual intuition, which gives them direct knowledge of (aspects of) the nature of ultimate reality. Kant's position is that the theoretical reason cannot go beyond the limits of human experience, and prove the existence of suprasensible beings such as God: nor can there be direct intuition of such beings. In the *Critique of Pure Reason*, he also provides a detailed refutation of the traditional arguments for God's existence: the ontological, cosmological and design or physico-theological arguments (see Glossary). So, we are dependent on the practical reason for what we can know of God and suprasensible reality. However, he warns that we must be careful not to try to erect metaphysical theories about God and ultimate reality on the basis of knowledge which we possess solely for moral purposes. We are concerned here with the practical reason; and the practical reason does not give us theoretical knowledge.

Kant's deontological ethics: the human desire for happiness cannot be the basis of morality

Kant once again emphasizes (Book I, Chapter III) his view that morality, which concerns what we ought to do, not what we are or want to do, cannot be based on any empirical factors, and that these include such human inclinations as the desire for happiness. Thus, Kantian ethics differs fundamentally from the consequentialist ethical theory of utilitarianism, which holds that pleasure/happiness is the only thing that is intrinsically or ultimately good, and that actions are right or wrong to the extent that they maximize or minimize pleasure/happiness. Kantian ethics are deontological: human beings have a duty to perform or not to perform certain actions, because they are right or wrong in themselves, irrespective of their consequences. Kant uses an example to illustrate his approach. An honest man is tempted to lie, in order to secure his short-term advantage and happiness. However, his practical reason judges that to do so would be wrong, and that he ought to tell the truth. Kant accepts that this does not mean that the practical reason condemns the human desire for happiness. On the contrary, happiness can assist morality: happy people may be more likely to behave morally than those distracted by unhappiness. However, pursuit of happiness is not a moral duty, and human beings must not allow the desire for it to guide their conduct. And, it is hard to disagree with Kant on this point. If there are absolute or objective standards of right and wrong, it will certainly make sense (it will not be self-contradictory) to say that it would be wrong to perform the action which is likely to produce most happiness, whether for the agent or others, or right to perform the action which is likely to produce least.

Human beings belong to both the world of sense and the world of understanding

In order to be able to obey the precepts of the moral law, and to be held responsible for any failure to do so, human beings must have absolute freedom of the will. But, how can they be free, when they are subject to the operation of laws of nature? Surely, like everything else in the world, their behaviour must be determined by natural necessity? This is what Kant calls the 'antinomy of pure speculative/theoretical reason'. As with his discussion of freedom in the *Groundwork*, Kant resolves this apparent contradiction by invoking the distinction between the world of sense and the world of understanding, to both of which human beings belong. The first is the world as it appears to us, due to the way that we, as human beings, experience it through our senses. As *phenomena* (appearances) in the world of sense, we are subject to the causal necessity of the laws of nature, and are not free. However, the second is the world as it is in itself. As rational beings, we are also *noumena* in this world, where, as free and rational beings, we are subject to moral laws which are independent of nature, which are grounded in reason and which we freely impose upon ourselves.

Two causalities

Kant develops his explanation in terms of two types of causality. The first, which governs the behaviour of things as appearances, subject to time in the world of sense, is natural necessity. The second, which concerns things in themselves in the world of understanding, is the causality of freedom, by which human beings, as rational beings, subject themselves to the precepts of the moral law. Without the second kind of causality, none of a rational being's actions would ever be under his control, and there would be no moral freedom. For example, if it were the case that natural necessity dictated that a thief perform his crime, he would be unable not to do it.

But, how can we be certain that this is not the case? Philosophers who are hard determinists (see Glossary) maintain that every human action is causally determined, so there is no such thing as human freedom or responsibility. Kant insists that it is because the moral law, which we all know about through our reason, tells us that the thief ought not to have committed the crime; and, as we all know that he ought not to have done it, we are able to say that he was also capable of not doing it.

No place for soft determinism

Kant dismisses what he calls a 'comparative concept of freedom': the kind of soft determinism proposed by David Hume, which seeks to reconcile freedom and natural necessity, by arguing that human beings are free, unless subject to external coercion. In his *Enquiry*, Hume argues that, although human actions are undeniably connected with human motives, and that the first follows the second, free will just means individuals being free to act, or not to act, according to the determination of their will. Thus, there is no such thing as human freedom, when it is opposed to causal necessity, not external constraint. For Kant, this comparative freedom is not good enough. To be free, human beings must have what we might call 'hard freedom': they must have a genuine choice as to whether or not to perform an action. If human freedom just means actions which originate in their desires, then human beings have the same freedom as the hands of a clock. Actions which are determined by a previous state, even if it is an internal one, are still determined by natural necessity, ruling out genuine moral freedom and responsibility. Kant invokes conscience as further proof of moral freedom. However ingenious our arguments for the inevitability of our immoral conduct, we know we are capable of not doing it, and we condemn the behaviour even of those whose criminality seems unalterable and congenital, as we believe that they have the power of choice and deserve punishment.

Would the existence of God limit human freedom?

But what if an all-knowing and all-powerful God, such as that of Christianity, created the world? This belief seems to threaten human freedom, by portraying human beings as mere puppets, made and worked by the supreme master. In his *Freedom of the Will*, the American theologian Jonathan Edwards makes out a powerful case for human moral freedom being incompatible with God's omniscience:

> To suppose the future volitions of moral agents not to be necessary events; or, which is the same thing, events which it is not impossible but that they may not come to pass; and yet to suppose that God certainly foreknows them, and knows all things; is to suppose God's knowledge to be inconsistent with itself. (p. 75)

Again, Kant turns to the difference between the worlds of sense and understanding. Time and causality belong to the world of sense, not the world of understanding. They are part of how we see and interpret the world, not part of things as they are in themselves. God is not the cause of actions in the world of sense, but of our existence as free things-in-themselves. Therefore, we can reconcile the causality we experience in the world, to which we are subject, with our freedom, by appreciating the distinction between the world of sense and world of understanding, to which we belong as rational beings.

A complicating factor in Kant's philosophy

Kant's distinction between the world of sense and the world of understanding complicates his moral philosophy, because it involves regarding human beings as both free and subject to the causal necessity of laws of nature. However, it is essential to his philosophical approach, because, while human beings clearly are subject to laws of nature, Kant's conception of moral responsibility requires human freedom to obey, or not to obey, the categorical imperatives of the moral law (the imperatives of morality, which command unconditionally). Kant accepts that the claim that human beings are free seems to contradict the natural necessity to which they are subject in the world of sense, and cannot be proved. But, for Kant, the idea of freedom cannot be given up, so it just has to be accepted that there actually is no contradiction between holding that beings, who are subject to laws of nature, are also independent of them, and subject to moral laws, given by pure reason. Again, it could be argued that this 'two-worlds' interpretation fits in with our actual experience of moral decision-making. We do find ourselves being impelled by our desires or fears towards actions that would contravene moral principles; but are also conscious of being capable of choosing not to perform them, even if we in fact do so.

Trying to comprehend the fundamental nature of reality

In both its speculative and practical functions (Book II, Chapter I), reason always tries to comprehend the fundamental nature of reality. However, as Kant has explained, human beings experience things in a certain way, because of the kind of beings they are. We derive our concepts of things from the information we receive through our senses, but this is conditioned by the way we experience them. Therefore, we have access, not to things/the world as they are in themselves (*noumena*), but to things/the world as they appear to us, or appearances (*phenomena*).

The highest good and avoiding heteronomy of the will

This not only imposes strict limits on what we can know, but gives rise to the illusion of regarding the appearances of things as if they are things in themselves. The urge to explore this illusion, in order to try to remove it, has advantages, as well as drawbacks, as it can give us an insight into a higher, unchangeable order of things, and enable us to understand how we ought to conduct ourselves. However, we must not lose sight of the fact that the basis for determining the will, and of making moral choices, does not lie in our inclinations, but in the commands of the moral law. But, even when human beings appreciate this, they still seek the highest or maximum good, in which performance of duty is rewarded by proportionate happiness. But, how does this relate to obeying the moral law? Kant goes on to discuss the highest good in the next chapter, but, before doing so, he stresses the point that we must not make pursuit of the highest good, which includes the search for happiness, the determining basis of the will. To avoid heteronomy of the will – the will being determined by human inclinations and desires, leading to spurious moral principles – our conduct must not be governed by anything other than the precepts of the moral law.

An ambiguity in the concept of the highest good

Kant explains (Chapter II) that the concept of the highest good is, in fact, ambiguous. It can mean either the supreme good, or the whole or complete good. There is no doubt that virtue, that is, worthiness of being happy, as a result of obeying the moral law for its own sake, is the supreme good for all rational beings, and the condition of the possibility of their pursuing happiness; but it is not the complete good. This requires happiness as well, with human beings receiving it, exactly in proportion to the degree that they have been virtuous.

Kant also acknowledges that, in the concept of the highest good for human beings, virtue and proportionate happiness are always thought of as linked together necessarily. But, how are they linked? What is the basis of their connection? It is certainly not analytic. It does not arise, as the Stoics and Epicureans (see Glossary) had mistakenly believed, because the concept of virtue includes that of happiness, or vice versa, such that to assert the presence of one, but not the other, is self-contradictory. Both groups of ancient Greek philosophers had failed to understand that the connection between virtue and happiness is synthetic: they are separate elements of the highest good.

A priori *synthetic propositions*

If the necessary connection between virtue and happiness is not analytic, but synthetic, this suggests that knowledge of it must also be *a posteriori*: that is, based on experience. Most modern philosophers believe that synthetic propositions (those which convey actual information) are so because they are based on empirical observation of the world. *A priori* propositions, on the other hand, which do not involve experience, are analytic: their truth can be established simply by analysing a concept or checking a definition. However, Kant does not share this view. He believes that propositions can be both synthetic and *a priori*. He does not accept the view that, to be synthetic, and to convey actual information (as here, about the connection between virtue and happiness), a proposition must also be *a posteriori*: that is, based on sense experience. He holds that there are *a priori* synthetic propositions, such as moral laws or principles, which tell human beings what they ought to do, and therefore give them actual information, but which derive, not from experience, but from the reason: the necessary connection between virtue and happiness is one of these. And, indeed, it is not clear how moral propositions could have an empirical basis. They are not concerned with how human beings actually behave, or what they desire to do, which could be established empirically, but with what rational beings ought to do.

The antinomy of practical reason

The necessary connection between virtue and happiness means that one leads to, or brings about, the other. But, exactly how? Kant (Chapter II, I) draws attention to an antinomy or contradiction, which is discovered by the practical reason. Human beings' idea of the highest good involves a necessary connection between virtue and happiness; but, this necessary connection could mean either that the human desire for happiness is the motive for behaving morally, or that moral behaviour leads to happiness. The first interpretation is unacceptable, for, if human beings were to behave morally, only in order to satisfy their desire for happiness, their motivation would be wrong: they would not be obeying the moral law for its own sake, but for what they could gain from doing so: happiness. However, the second interpretation also seems impossible, because, in this world, happiness does not necessarily follow complete compliance with the precepts of the moral law: virtuous people often do not receive the happiness they deserve.

In fact, Kant explains (Chapter II, II), like the antinomy of pure speculative reason, (see above) the antinomy or contradiction or pure practical reason is not a true one. With the former, the apparent contradiction between the necessity of natural laws, to which human beings are subject, and the absolute freedom required by the moral law and moral responsibility, was resolved by the distinction between human membership of both the world of sense and the world of understanding. When the world and its events are viewed only as appearances, we can see that human beings, as *phenomena* in the world of sense, are subject to natural causality, but, as *noumena*, in the world of understanding, they are free and not subject to any natural law.

It is the same with the antinomy of pure practical reason. Although pursuit of happiness is not the basis for behaving morally, the idea that virtue necessarily leads to happiness is only false, if thought of as a form of causality in the world of sense, and on the assumption that human beings' only existence, as rational beings, is in this world. When we think of ourselves as *noumena*, in the world of understanding, we can see the possibility that, through God, the creator of world, there may be a necessary connection between morality and happiness, sufficient for attainment of the highest good. Our error is to think that this necessary connection exists in the world of sense.

Being pleased when we act morally

It is all too easy to be mistaken about the basis of moral conduct. While a virtuous human being will not find joy in his life, unless he knows himself to be virtuous, the happiness he experiences is not a motive for moral conduct. Human beings tend to confuse the necessary connection between a moral attitude and awareness that our will is directly determined by the moral law with the fact that we are pleased with the resulting actions. However, it is reason alone, not pleasure, which determines the will, and thus gives rise to the pleasure. We must take care not to degrade the proper incentive to action, the moral law itself, by confusing it with pleasant feelings, or perform our duty, not for the sake of the moral law, but for the agreeable feelings we experience from doing so. Kant suggests that we call the pleasant feelings, produced by our consciousness of virtue, 'self-satisfaction', rather than 'happiness'.

Overcoming, and not acting from, inclinations

Being free and aware of our ability to obey the moral law makes us independent of our inclinations as motivating causes. Indeed (Kant maintains), our inclinations, which vary in strength, according to how far we give in to them, are a constant trial to rational beings. Further, although positive and unselfish inclinations, such as sympathy and compassion, can assist morality, by encouraging an individual to do his duty, they cannot produce moral maxims. Indeed, they can lead to moral confusion, if they are allowed to become the determining basis for performance of duty. Kant's point is that consequences are not enough: motive also matters. Our motive for helping others must not be the inclination we feel, at this moment, to do so, but recognition that it is a duty that the moral law always places upon us. And, of course, our feeling that we would like to help x, in this particular situation, today, may not arise in relation to y, in a different situation, tomorrow: but, the moral law's requirement that it is our duty to help others applies today, tomorrow and every day.

Not putting the cart before the horse

Resolving the antinomy of pure practical reason means that we can regard a necessary connection between morality and happiness as possible. However, happiness cannot lead to morality, so the latter is the supreme good, and the primary condition of the highest good, while happiness is merely its second element and a (necessary) consequence of morality. While reason requires us to regard attainment of the highest good as possible, it also requires us to regard the necessary connection between morality and happiness, not as part of the world of sense, but as part of the suprasensible relation of things. However, the practical consequences of this relation, actions aimed at realizing the highest good, do belong to, and are to be performed in, the world of sense.

The relationship of practical reason and theoretical reason

Kant explores (Chapter II, III) the relationship between reason in its two applications. In particular, is it the case that practical reason is only able to work on what it receives from theoretical reason? No, because practical reason has its own, original *a priori* moral principles. Nor is theoretical reason entitled to reject practical reason's propositions, on the grounds that they cannot be authenticated empirically: they do not contradict reason, while they provide information which is inaccessible to theoretical reason. Practical reason and theoretical reason are two uses of the same reason. Neither has overall primacy over the other: each has primacy in its own sphere, the former in *a priori* matters, which include morality.

The immortality of the soul as a postulate of pure practical reason

The necessary object of a will, which conforms to the moral law, is to bring about the highest good in the world: happiness in proportion to moral virtue. However, human beings are subject to interests and inclinations, many of which impel them to act in ways which contravene the moral law. This is why, for human beings, unlike angels, the precepts of the moral law have to be expressed as a series of imperatives, which they are commanded to obey. While attainment of the highest good is possible, the supreme condition of attaining it is moral perfection, a will that is completely adequate to the moral law, and which does not need to be commanded, in order to obey it.

Kant explains (Chapter II, IV) that this is holiness of the will, which human beings cannot achieve, during their lives. If they are going to achieve it, there must be infinite progress towards it, beyond the limits of mortal existence. Therefore, the practical reason must assume an indefinite continuation of their existence and personalities, which is immortality of the soul. Immortality is inseparably linked with the moral law, and must be regarded as a postulate (necessary condition) of pure practical reason. However, it cannot be proved theoretically. What human beings may hope for is a share in the highest good, on the basis of endless progress from the morally worse to the morally better. In fact, Kant does not foresee a point when human beings will actually achieve holiness of the will, but immortality is their only hope of doing so.

The existence of God as a postulate of pure practical reason

Postulation of immortality solves the problem of how human beings can attain moral perfection. But, how is the proportioning of happiness to virtue to be achieved? As the moral law itself contains no basis for a necessary connection between them (Chapter II, V), the practical reason needs to postulate the existence of a cause, capable of producing this effect: a supreme cause of nature, God.

Kant is quick to point out the dangerous implications postulating God has for the autonomy of morality. Plato pinpoints the essence of this issue in his *Euthyphro*: is an action right because God wills it; or does God will it because it is right? For Kant, there is no question as to which it is: God's will cannot be regarded as the reason why human beings should obey the moral law, nor is God's existence required as the basis of moral obligation. Again, throughout his discussion of God's existence, Kant is careful to reject any idea that the hope of being rewarded with God-given happiness is a legitimate motive for moral behaviour. Morality is independent of God, and the supreme good for all rational beings is to be worthy of happiness, through obeying the moral law for its own sake; but their complete good requires happiness, and therefore the presupposition of the existence of God, to bring this about.

However, human nature being what it is, once the connection between moral conduct and happiness has been made, the second inevitably becomes a motive for the first, despite the fact that Kant is at pains to deny it. It is also easy to misinterpret, or misrepresent, his position, as suggesting that people should obey the moral law, in order to be (ultimately) happy.

Christian ethical teaching

Kant maintains that only Christian ethical teaching provides a concept of the highest good, which meets the strictest demands of practical reason. It is not heteronomous, as it makes God and his will the basis, not of the moral law, which is to be obeyed solely from duty, but only of achieving the highest good. Through the idea of highest good, as the object of pure practical reason (Kant argues), the moral law leads to religion: that is, to recognition of all duties as divine commands. However, Christian ethical teaching does not present fear (of God's displeasure) or hope (of divine rewards) as incentives for moral conduct, as this would destroy the moral worth of actions. In relation to the holiness of morals that Christian teaching requires, all the moral law offers human beings is infinite progress towards it, together with the hope of that progress continuing indefinitely. However, Christian ethical teaching portrays human beings' total obedience to the moral law as a kingdom of God, in which nature and morals are harmonized. So, in this world, rational beings have moral holiness as a standard, but will not necessarily be happy, however moral they are: happiness in proportion to their morality, which is bliss, is an object of hope, which they can attain only in eternity, with God's assistance.

God's purpose in creating the world

Kant points out that their being unequal to their duty is the
only limit on the happiness that a wise and all-powerful God
is able to distribute to rational beings. Further, his ultimate
purpose in creating the world is not to ensure their happiness, but the highest good, which involves their being worthy
of it. However, nothing glorifies God more than the holy duty
that the moral law, which is also his holy law, imposes on us
being completed by his giving us happiness in proportion to
our fulfilment of it. Of course, Kant is not interested in any
alternative Christian beliefs about God or God's purpose in
creating the world. Christian teaching is made to fit in with
his moral philosophy.

No extension of theoretical knowledge

It seems then that, although, in its theoretical use, reason is
unable to discover anything about God, including his existence, in its practical use, it is able to provide a lot of information. However, Kant insists (Chapter II, VI) that God, immortality and freedom are postulated, in order to make sense of
morality: postulating immortality derives from the practical
necessity of human beings' existence being sufficiently long
to fulfil the moral law; postulating freedom from the necessity for human beings to be independent of the world of sense,
and able to determine their will according to the law of the
world of understanding; and postulating God from the necessity of there being one who is capable of making attainment
of the highest good possible. Therefore, the 'knowledge' we
acquire from the practical reason is solely for moral purposes,
and so it does not give us theoretical knowledge of what the

soul, the world of understanding (where we are free), or God are like in themselves.

Knowledge for purely practical purposes

Kant does concede (Chapter II, VII) that there is a limited addition to theoretical knowledge. It is increased, but only in the sense that concepts (of freedom, immortality and God), which could previously only be thought about, are now affirmed to exist. The postulates gain objective reality, because they are necessary conditions of our ability to make what the moral law demands our object, and to attain the highest good; and reason, in its theoretical use, is compelled to acknowledge their existence, although it cannot completely comprehend or explain them. Further, theoretical reason recognizes that the postulates cannot be used for purely speculative purposes, and acts to prevent their becoming a source of superstition or fanaticism. Kant's prime concern is to rule out employment of the postulates for metaphysical speculation of the kind he refutes in the *Critique of Pure Reason*, or their use as a basis for claiming that there can be empirical knowledge of supra-sensible objects.

The futility of natural theology

Kant then directs his fire at the efforts of natural theology (the use of reason/experience to establish God's existence and/or attributes) to understand God's nature and develop a theory of suprasensible beings. When asked to discuss God's characteristics, such as his understanding or will, all natural theologians can offer, once the anthropomorphic elements have been removed from their arguments, are mere words. Does (Kant asks) the concept of God belong to physics, metaphysics or morality? God is not part of physics, because we can have no theoretical concept of a being, who does not exist in the world of sense, to which our theoretical knowledge is limited: we cannot draw any inferences from what we know of this world to the idea of God, or prove that he exists. To be able to say, with certainty, that this world is possible only if God has created it, would require omniscience on our part, and knowledge of all possible worlds, to compare them with this one.

God is not part of metaphysics either, because we cannot know, or prove, that God exists merely from the concept of God, in the way that the ontological argument (see Glossary) tries to do. All we can infer, from the order, purposiveness and size of the world, is that its maker or designer is wise, kind and powerful (design argument: see Glossary), but this does not yield what the metaphysicians seek: an all-knowing, all-loving and all-powerful cause of the world. While it may seem reasonable (and is also desirable) to ascribe every perfection to the cause of the world, this would go well beyond an inference from what we know of the world. If we confine ourselves to what we can know empirically, God is an imprecisely determined concept, and metaphysical speculation tells us nothing.

So, morality is the key?

However (Kant concludes), it is different with morality. In order for attainment of the highest good to be possible, God must have every perfection. He must be omniscient, to penetrate to the innermost attitudes underlying our conduct; omnipotent, to apportion appropriate consequences to it; and also omnipresent and eternal.

However, even those who agree with Kant that there are moral laws, which we must obey for their own sake, and that we have duties to other rational beings as ends in themselves (and who may also agree with him that there must be absolute freedom, if there is to be moral responsibility), may reject his view that God and immortality are necessary, in order that rational beings may (eventually) attain the highest good. They may argue that the necessary connection between moral conduct and happiness is just a hope or an illusion. There simply is no such connection. We must do our duty, and not look for anything else. Some virtuous people will be happy in this world; others will not be; and that's just the way it is. On the other hand, despite the numerous warnings he gives, there will be those who focus exclusively on the fact that Kant has provided some sort of proof of the existence of God and immortality, and ignore the way that they are related to his moral theory.

So, is this an argument for God's existence?

And, Kant's claim that God is a necessary postulate of the practical reason is sometimes described as a 'moral argument' for God's existence. However, what he gives us, in the *Critique of Practical Reason*, is not a formal, theoretical proof of God's existence, to replace the traditional arguments which he has refuted in the *Critique of Pure Reason*, but reasons for believing that, without God, the moral picture would be incomplete:

> It consists of the claim that anyone seriously committed to respect moral values as exercising a claim upon his life, must thereby implicitly believe in the reality of a transhuman source and basis for these values. (Hick, p. 27)

Again, Hastings Rashdall poses the question of where, if there is 'an unconditional, objectively valid, Moral Law', of the kind Kant describes in the *Groundwork* and the *Critique of Practical Reason*, 'such an ideal exists' (Rashdall, p. 149). His answer is that it can exist:

> ... nowhere and nohow but in a mind: an absolute moral ideal can exist only in a Mind from which all Reality is derived. Our moral ideal can only claim objective validity in so far as it can rationally be regarded as the revelation of a moral ideal eternally existing in the mind of God. (Rashdall, p. 150)

The problem with Hick's and Rashdall's interpretations of Kant's 'moral argument' is that they can so easily compromise the independence of morality that Kant is so concerned to preserve, and give the impression that God is not only necessary for completing the moral picture, and ensuring happiness in proportion to moral desert, but as a basis of moral obligation as such.

The possibility of happiness

Although our moral duty (Chapter II, VIII) is grounded in the moral law alone, which does not need to be reinforced by belief in or fear of God, it is legitimate for us to strive for the highest good, and for ultimate happiness in proportion to our moral worth: and, to be an object of our striving, such happiness must also be attainable. It is impossible to prove that this allocation cannot occur through laws of nature, but reason is unable to accept that it can, and postulates the existence of God.

The benefits of the limitations of knowledge

Our lives are a constant battle between the urgings of our inclinations and desires and the precepts of the moral law. However, Kant points out (Chapter II, IX), we can conceive of a different situation. Instead of the current conflict, which develops moral strength, we could have complete theoretical knowledge and constant awareness of God's majesty and eternity. We would then obey the moral law, not for its own sake, but from fear of the consequences of not doing so. Our motive would be wrong, and our actions would lack moral worth. But, as things are, our view of ultimate reality is obscure and ambiguous, and we can only conjecture that God exists. As this is the only sort of environment in which we can develop a truly moral attitude, God is to be praised as much for what he has withheld from us, as for what he has revealed to us.

Moral education

Kant offers (Part II) some interesting suggestions about how genuine moral attitudes can be established and developed. Educators should capitalize on young people's willingness to examine and discuss moral questions. Having taught their pupils the precepts of the moral law, they should search history for examples of the duties they have taught being put into practice, and encourage their pupils to assess the moral value of the actions concerned. This will develop their pupils' ability to assess the morality of conduct, and lay the foundations of their future moral probity. What they should not do is commend the unattainable perfection displayed by the heroes of novels, which only encourages exaggerated feelings and neglect of duty. Indeed, Kant deprecates the cultivation of tender feelings, which can result in actions motivated by emotion, rather than duty. An action must be performed solely for the sake of the moral law, not because of inclinations, including those of sympathy and compassion.

Conclusion

Kant concludes the *Critique of Practical Reason* with a particularly moving passage:

> Two things fill the mind with ever new and increasing admiration and reverence, the more frequently and persistently one's meditation deals with them: *the starry sky above me and the moral law within me.* (p. 203)

He explains that the first, which begins from our position in the external world of sense, minimizes our importance, making us seem mere dots in the universe. However, the second, which begins from the invisible self, raises our worth infinitely, for the moral law discloses the life of a rational being, whose existence, which is not restricted by the 'conditions and boundaries of this life', continues to infinity.

Assessment

Throughout the *Groundwork*, Kant stresses the autonomy of morality, and that the moral law is to be obeyed for its own sake, not because of inclinations or for the sake of any external factor. Then, in the *Critique of Practical Reason*, he brings God into the picture, and seems to contradict all that he has said previously. But, this is not the case. We must be clear what

Kant is saying. Postulating God's existence does not compromise the autonomy of morality. The moral law is to be obeyed for its own sake: and God is not needed, either to provide the content of morality, or to make human beings recognize or perform their duty. Moral laws do not come from God, nor do they depend upon him in any way.

However, although morality is independent of God and religion, Kant points out that human beings have an idea of the highest good, in which they not only do their duty, but are rewarded for doing so by proportionate happiness. Indeed (he maintains), there is an ambiguity in the concept of the 'highest good': it can mean the 'supreme good', which is worthiness of being happy, through obeying the moral law for its own sake, or the 'complete good', which requires happiness as well.

This does not mean that human beings should be moral because they hope to be rewarded by happiness: this would compromise the autonomy of morality, by making (the desire for) happiness a motive for being moral. Rather, it is to recognize that those who are moral deserve to be happy. As David Ross puts it, Kant acknowledges that, although only virtue is morally good, happiness which is deserved because of virtue, is not just a 'source of satisfaction to its possessor, but objectively good' (*The Right and the Good*, p. 136). Clearly, virtue is not always rewarded by deserved happiness in this world, so, like freedom, God, and also immortality, are necessary postulates of the practical reason. Without freedom, there could not be moral responsibility; without God, to apportion happiness to moral desert, the complete good would not be attainable; and, without immortality, human beings would lack the opportunity to achieve moral perfection, or to receive the happiness their moral conduct merits.

Some Key Quotations

The Analytic of Pure Practical Reason

. . . the distinction of the *doctrine of happiness* from the *doctrine of morals*, in the first of which empirical principles amount to the whole foundation whereas in the second they amount not even to the slightest addition to it, is the first and most important enterprise incumbent upon the Analytic of Pure Practical Reason. (p. 118)

Morality and happiness

. . . pure practical reason does not want us to *give up* our claims to happiness . . . only that as soon as duty is at issue we take *no account* of them . . . furtherance of one's happiness can never directly be a duty . . . since all determining bases of the will except for the single pure practical law of reason (the moral law) are . . . empirical and . . . belong to the principle of happiness, they must . . . be separated from the supreme moral principle and never be incorporated in it . . . (p. 119)

Necessity and freedom

The concept of causality as *natural necessity*, as distinguished from causality as *freedom*, concerns only the existence of things insofar as it is *determinable in time* and consequently [of things] as appearances, in contrast to their causality as things in themselves . . . no other path remains than to attribute the existence of a thing insofar as it is determinable in time, and hence also the [thing's] causality according to the law of *natural necessity, merely to appearance*, but to attribute *freedom to the same being as a thing in itself.* (pp. 120–1)

Absolute freedom and moral responsibility

Without this freedom . . . no moral law is possible . . . if the

freedom of our will were none other than the latter ... (...
psychological and comparative freedom, not simultaneously
transcendental, i.e., absolute, freedom), then it would basic-
ally be no better than the freedom of a turnspit ... (p. 123)

We are still guilty
... the rational being can rightly say concerning every unlawful action which he commits that he could have omitted it,
even though as appearance it is sufficiently determined in the
past and is to this extent unfailingly necessary ... whatever
arises from one's power of choice ... has as its basis a free
causality ... These actions ... [are] the consequence of the
voluntarily assumed and immutable evil principles ... (pp.
124, 127)

God and freedom
Just as it would ... be a contradiction to say that God is a creator of appearances, so it is also a contradiction to say that as
creator he is the cause of the actions in the world of sense and
hence [of these actions] as appearances, even though he is the
cause of the existence of acting beings (as noumena) ... creation concerns their intelligible but not their sensible existence
and therefore cannot be regarded as determining bases of appearances ... (p. 130)

Two forms of causality
... the same action which, as belonging to the world of sense,
is always sensibly conditioned – i.e., mechanically necessary –
can yet at the same time, as [belonging] to the causality of the
acting being insofar as this belongs to the intelligible world,
also be based on a sensibly unconditioned causality and therefore be thought of as free. (p. 132)

The moral law and the highest good

... in point of the determination of the concept *of the high-est good* ... The moral law is the sole determining basis of the pure will ... although the highest good may indeed be the entire *object* of a pure practical reason ... it is not on that account to be considered the *determining basis* of that will, and the moral law alone must be regarded as the basis for making the highest good ... one's object. (pp. 139–40)

The supreme good and the complete good

The concept of the *highest* contains an ambiguity ... virtue (as the worthiness to be happy) is the *supreme condition* of whatever may seem to us desirable, and hence also of all our pursuit of happiness, and ... is therefore the *supreme* good ... But virtue is not ... the whole and complete good as the object of the power of desire of rational, finite beings. For ... that, *happiness* too is required (p. 141)

Virtue and happiness

In the highest good that is practical for us ... virtue and happiness are thought as necessarily linked, so that one cannot be assumed by pure practical reason without the other's belonging to it ... either the desire for happiness must be the motivating cause for maxims of virtue, or the maxim of virtue must be the efficient cause of happiness. The first is impossible *absolutely* ... the second is *impossible also* ... because ... no necessary connection, sufficient for the highest good, of happiness with virtue in the world can be expected ... through the most meticulous observance of moral laws. (pp. 144–5)

The world of sense and the world of understanding

... one and the same being acting *as appearance* ... has a

causality in the world of sense which always conforms to the mechanism of nature; but, with regard to the same event . . . as *noumenon* (as pure intelligence . . .), he can contain a determining basis . . . which is itself free from any natural law. (pp. 145–6)

Resolving the antinomy of pure practical reason

. . . that a virtuous attitude necessarily produces happiness, is false *not absolutely* but only insofar as this attitude is regarded as the form of causality in the world of sense . . . is false only *conditionally*. (p. 146)

The true incentive to action

. . . one must also be on guard against degrading . . . the proper and genuine incentive, the law itself . . . Only through this way of conceiving [respect], however, can one attain what one sees . . . that actions be done not merely in conformity with duty . . . but from duty . . . (p. 149)

Acting from the right motive

Even that feeling of sympathy and softhearted compassion if it precedes deliberation as to what . . . duty is and becomes a determining basis, is itself burdensome to right-minded persons, brings their deliberate maxims into confusion, and gives rise to the wish to be rid of them and subject solely to legislative reason. (p. 150)

Happiness is a secondary element of the highest good

. . . one can at least think as possible . . . a . . . necessary linkage between the consciousness of morality and . . . the expectation of a happiness proportionate to it . . . [but] pursuit of happiness cannot possibly produce morality . . . therefore, the *supreme* good (as the primary condition of the highest good) consists in morality, whereas happiness amounts ... to the second element of the highest good ... Only in this subordination is the *highest good* the entire object of pure practical reason. (p. 151)

Immortality of the soul

This infinite progression ... is possible only on the presupposition of an existence and personality – of the same rational being – continuing *ad infinitum* (which is called the immortality of the soul) ... the highest good is practically possible only on the presupposition of ... immortality ... and hence this ... as linked inseparably with the moral law is a *postulate* of pure practical reason...he [the rational being] can never hope to be fully adequate to God's will ... either here or at any foreseeable future point of time ... but can hope to be so only in the infinity of his continuance ... (pp. 155–7)

The existence of God

The moral law led ... to a practical problem ... the necessary completeness ... of the first and foremost part of the highest good, *morality*; and since this problem can be solved fully only in an eternity, it led to the postulate of *immortality*. The same law must also lead to the possibility of the second good ... *happiness* commensurate to that morality ... it must lead to ... a cause adequate to this effect ... it must postulate the *existence of God* ... (pp. 157–8)

God and morality

... the existence of a cause of nature as a whole, distinct from nature, which contains the basis of this connection ... of the exact harmony of ... happiness with ... morality is also *postu-*

lated . . . I . . . do not mean by this that it is necessary to assume the existence of God *as a basis of all obligation as such* (. . . this rests . . . solely on the autonomy of reason itself). (pp. 158–9)

Christian morality

. . . the Christian principle of *morality* . . . makes the cognition of God and of his will the basis not of these [moral] laws but only of . . . reaching the highest good under the condition of compliance . . . it posits even the proper *incentive* for compliance with them not in the wished-for consequences . . . but in the conception of duty alone . . . (p. 163)

God's purpose in creating the world

. . . if one inquires about *God's ultimate purpose* in creating the world, one must mention not the *happiness* of rational beings in the world but *the highest good*, which adds to that wish . . . the condition of being worthy of happiness . . . the *morality* of these same rational beings . . . nothing glorifies God more than . . . observance of the holy duty that his law imposes on us . . . [being] supplemented by his splendid provision to crown such a beautiful order with commensurate happiness. (pp. 165–6)

The postulates of the practical reason

. . . is our cognition actually expanded . . . by pure practical reason . . . *only for a practical aim* . . . we thereby cognize neither the nature of our soul, nor the intelligible world, nor the supreme being as to what they are in themselves, but . . . only . . . in the *practical* concept *of the highest good* as the object of our will . . . (p. 169)

The limits of knowledge

. . . it is now also easy to find the answer to this important question: *whether the concept of God is one belonging to physics* (hence also to metaphysics . . .) . . . *or one belonging to morality* . . . in order to say that this world was possible only through a *God* . . . we would have to cognize . . . all possible worlds (so as to be able to compare them with this one), and hence would have to be omniscient . . . to cognize the existence of this being altogether from mere concepts is absolutely impossible . . . on the empirical path (of physics) the concept of God remains always a *concept* . . . (With metaphysics . . . nothing at all can be accomplished). (pp. 175–7)

Moral conflict and the truly moral attitude

. . . instead of the conflict that the moral attitude now has to carry on with the inclinations . . . *God* and *eternity* with their *dreadful majesty* would lie unceasingly *before our eyes* . . . Transgression of the law would indeed be avoided . . . [but] most lawful actions would be done from fear . . . none at all from duty; and a moral worth of actions . . . would not exist at all. The conduct of human beings . . . would thus be converted into a mere mechanism . . . as in a puppet show . . . (pp. 185–6)

Moral education

I do not know why educators of the youth have not long since made use of this propensity of reason to enter with gratification upon even the subtlest examination when practical questions are raised; and . . . have not searched through the biographies of ancient and modern times . . . for . . . supporting instances by which to activate . . . their pupils' judgment in noting the lesser or greater moral import of such actions. (p. 193)

The holiness of duty

... to put everything second to the holiness of duty alone and to become conscious that one *can* do this because our own reason acknowledges it as its command and says that one *ought* to do it – this is ... to elevate oneself entirely above the world of sense ... (p. 199)

Looking outwards and inwards

Two things fill the mind with ever new and increasing admiration and reverence, the more frequently and persistently one's meditation deals with them: *the starry sky above me and the moral law within me* ... The first sight, of a countless multitude of worlds, annihilates ... my importance as an *animal creature* ... The second sight ... elevates infinitely my worth as that of an *intelligence* by my personality, in which the moral law reveals to me a life independent of animality and ... the entire world of sense ... (p. 203)

Suggestions for Further Reading

Immanuel Kant, *Critique of Pure Reason*, ed. M. Gregor, Cambridge: Cambridge University Press, 1997.

Immanuel Kant, *Critique of Practical Reason*, trans. W. S. Pluhar, Indianapolis/Cambridge: Hackett Publishing Company, 2002.

Immanuel Kant, *Groundwork of the Metaphysics of Morals*, ed. M. Gregor, Cambridge: Cambridge University Press, 1997.

Immanuel Kant, *Religion within the Boundaries of Mere Reason*, ed. A. Wood and G. di Giovanni, Cambridge: Cambridge University Press, 1998.

Basic Writings of Saint Thomas Aquinas, vol. I, ed. A. C. Pegis, Indianapolis/Cambridge: Hackett Publishing Company,

1997 (contains the *Summa Theologica*, Part I) (Question II, Third Article).

Anselm, *Proslogion with the Replies of Gaunilo and Anselm*, trans. T. Williams, Indianapolis/Cambridge: Hackett Publishing Company, 2001 (Chapters II–IV).

F. Copleston, *A History of Philosophy*, vol. 6, Part II (Kant), New York, NY: Image Books, 1964 (Chapter 14).

R. Descartes, *Discourse on Method and Meditations on First Philosophy*, trans. D. A. Cress, fourth edition, Indianapolis/Cambridge: Hackett Publishing Company, 1998 (Meditation V).

J. Edwards, *A Careful and Strict Enquiry Into The Modern Prevailing Notions Of That Freedom Of The Will*, New York, NY: Leavitt and Allen, 1852, reprinted by Whitefish, MT: Kessinger Publishing, 2007.

J. Hick, *Philosophy of Religion*, Englewood Cliffs, NJ: Prentice-Hall, 1963.

D. Hume, *An Enquiry Concerning Human Understanding*, ed. T. L. Beauchamp, Oxford and New York: Oxford University Press, 2000 (Section 8).

D. Hume, *Dialogues Concerning Natural Religion*, ed. R. H. Popkin, second edition, Indianapolis/Cambridge: Hackett Publishing Company, 1998.

R. Johnson, 'Kant's Moral Philosophy' (revised 2008), in E. N. Zalta (ed.), *Stanford Encyclopaedia of Philosophy* at http://plato.stanford.edu.

M. Kuehn, *Kant: A Biography*, Cambridge: Cambridge University Press, 1998.

O. O'Neill, 'Kantian Ethics', in P. Singer (ed.), *A Companion to Ethics*, Cambridge: Cambridge University Press, 1993.

H. J. Paton, *The Categorical Imperative*, Philadelphia: University of Philadelphia Press, 1971.

Suggestions for Further Reading

Plato, *Defence of Socrates, Euthyphro and Crito*, trans. and ed.
D. Gallop, Oxford and New York: Oxford University Press,
1997.

Plato, *The Republic*, trans. H. D. P. Lee, second edition (revised
and reissued with new Further Reading), London: Penguin,
2003 (Part VII).

H. Rashdall, *The Theory of Good and Evil* in J. Hick (ed.), *The
Existence of God*, New York, NY: Macmillan, 1964.

W. D. Ross, *The Right and the Good*, Oxford: Oxford University
Press, 1930.

P. Rossi, 'Kant's Philosophy of Religion' (revised 2005), in
E. N. Zalta (ed.), *Stanford Encyclopaedia of Philosophy*, at
http://plato.stanford.edu.

R. J. Sullivan, *Immanuel Kant's Moral Theory*, Cambridge:
Cambridge University Press, 1989.

Detailed Summary of Immanuel Kant's *Critique of Practical Reason (The Concept of the Highest Good and the Postulates of the Practical Reason)*

Part I   Doctrine of the Elements of Pure Practical Reason
Book I   Analytic of Pure Practical Reason
From Chapter III   Critical Examination of the Analytic of Pure Practical Reason (pp. 114–35)

The 'critical examination' of a 'science' is investigating and justifying its particular 'systematic form' (p. 114). Now, both '**practical**' and '*pure reason*' are based on the same '**cognitive power**', so, to pinpoint the difference between them, they must be compared (p. 114). 'Pure theoretical reason' starts with objects that are given to the 'understanding', and thus with '**sensibility**' (what we can learn through the senses), and then moves to 'concepts' and '*principles*' (p. 114). The practical reason, on the other hand, is concerned, not with knowledge of objects, but with the '*will*', which involves '**causality**' and the 'power' to make things '*actual*' (p. 114). The practical reason starts with the '*possibility*' of the '*practical a priori principles*' of the moral law, and moves from them to 'objects', in order to categorize them as 'good or evil', in accordance with these principles (pp. 114–15).

*****

Is 'pure reason', without the introduction of any '**empirical**' **elements**, 'practical by itself alone' (p. 116)? We can establish, from the '*commonest practical use of reason*', that the '**supreme practical principle**', which every 'human reason' recognizes as the 'supreme law of its will', is wholly '*a priori*' and does not depend on 'sensible data' (p. 116). We have only to appeal to the 'judgement of common human understanding', because anything 'empirical', which becomes a '**determining basis' of maxims**, is instantly detectable, due to the feelings of satisfaction or pain that accompany it (p. 117). However, this not the case where the determining basis is 'rational' (p. 117). Whereas we have no 'respect' for 'inclinations', we do for the moral law, and we understand that we can never 'be required to *obey* any law other than the **pure practical law of reason**' (pp. 117–8).

Distinguishing the '*doctrine of happiness*', which is wholly founded on '**empirical** principles', from the '*doctrine of morals*', to which they add nothing, is the difficult primary task of the '**Analytic** of the Pure Practical Reason' (p. 118). However, in relation to anyone's 'practical reason', the 'philosopher' can use examples to illustrate the difference between the moral law and empirical factors as the 'determining' bases of actions (p. 118). Any generally honest man, faced with the temptation to lie for his own short-term 'advantage' and happiness, can recognize the 'worthlessness' of doing so, such that his 'practical reason' judges what he 'ought' to do, and combines with his self-respect to indicate that he should be truthful (pp. 118–19). This does not mean that pure practical reason wishes us to repudiate all 'claims to happiness'; only that, where 'duty' is concerned, we must not be guided by them (p. 119). Indeed, it can be our duty to promote our own happiness, as its accompaniments, such as 'skill, health' or 'wealth', may help us to perform our duty, whereas the unhappiness of 'poverty', for example, may distract us from doing so (p. 119). However, pursuit of happiness is not a direct duty; so, we must distinguish it from, and never incorporate it into, the 'supreme moral principle' of the moral law, as this would eliminate 'all moral worth' (p. 119).

If we could gain 'insight' into the 'possibility' of an **efficient cause**'s 'freedom', we would also recognize, not just the possibility, but the 'necessity' of the moral law as rational beings' 'supreme **practical law**', given that we ascribe **freedom of the will** to them: for '**practical freedom**' is the will's 'independence' of anything other than the moral law (p. 119). And, as this 'insight' is not achievable in the '**world of sense**', we are fortunate that the moral law compels us to 'assume' this freedom (pp. 119–20). However, there are those who persist in trying to explain our freedom through 'empirical principles', thus limiting it to the world of sense (p. 120). They thus deny the pure practical reason's 'splendid' revelation to us of the '**transcendent concept of freedom**'; and, indeed, 'annul the moral law itself' (p. 120). So, we need to demonstrate the 'shallowness' of '*empiricism*' (p. 120).

'Causality' as '*natural necessity*' is to do with things as 'appearances', which are '*determinable in time*'; it is not the 'causality' of '*freedom*', which is to do with 'things in themselves' (p. 120). However, if the second is considered to be the same as the first, none of my actions would ever be '*under my control*' (p. 120). Everything I did would be determined by what preceded it in time, and so subject to a '**steady chain of nature**' (p. 121). Therefore, if we wish to regard 'a being' whose existence is 'determined in time' as free, we cannot exempt him completely from 'natural necessity', without ascribing what he does to 'blind chance' (p. 121). But, if natural necessity applies to these beings as '*things in themselves*', there would be no freedom

41

(p. 121). So, we must conclude that the same being is subject to natural necessity, as an *'appearance'*, but is free as a **'thing in itself'** and a member of the world of understanding (p. 121).

Let us take someone who steals. If he performs this action, according to natural necessity, it cannot be 'left undone'; so, how can we say that it could have been, because the moral law declares that it 'ought to have been' (p. 121)? It is 'pitiful' to try to argue that a person is simultaneously free and subject to natural necessity, by introducing a **'comparative concept of freedom'** (p. 122). The argument is that a 'free action' is one that is determined *'internally'*, and which, as it originates from our 'desires', is 'at our own discretion' (p. 122). On this basis, a clock's 'motion' would be free, as it moves its own hands (p. 122). It makes no difference whether the 'determining bases' of our actions are internal or external (p. 122). If the 'basis of their existence' is in a *'previous state'*, then, even if they are 'psychological', not 'mechanical', they are still **'necessitating conditions of past time'**, which are not under the agent's *'control'*, and so rule out **'transcendental freedom'** and the possibility of the 'moral law' (pp. 122–3). If our freedom is only 'comparative', not 'absolute', it is no better than that 'of a turnspit', which, once 'wound up', 'performs its motions on its own' (p. 123).

However, as well as being subject to the 'conditions of time', the individual also thinks of himself as not subject to them, and as determined solely by laws that he 'gives to himself through reason'; and so as a **'noumenon'** in the **world of understanding**, as well as an appearance (p. 124). From this standpoint, the 'rational being' is able to maintain his independence of the world of sense, and so is capable of not performing his 'every unlawful action', despite its being 'determined in the past' and, to that degree, 'unfailingly necessary' (p. 124).

And, our '**conscience**' upholds this view (p. 124). However ingeniously we argue for the inevitability of our 'unlawful behaviour', the 'prosecutor' within us is aware that, with the use of this 'freedom', we could not have done it (pp. 124–5). We try to excuse ourselves by pleading bad habits, but cannot avoid 'self-censure'; and this gives rise to the pain of '**repentance**' (p. 125). As the deed is past, there is a sense in which this is pointless, but, where the moral law is concerned, our reason takes no account of time, but only enquires whether the deed is ours. If our 'insight' into human beings' 'way of thinking' was so profound as to enable us to understand all the incentives which produce actions, such that we could foresee all future actions, we could still maintain human freedom; for there can be no 'physical explanation' of the individual's 'spontaneity' as a 'thing in itself' (pp. 125–6). Take those people who, from 'childhood', exhibit every characteristic of growing 'villainy', and the absence of any capacity for 'improvement' (p. 126). Despite the apparently 'hopeless' condition of 'their minds', we condemn their actions, and we would not do so, unless we believed that 'immutable evil principles' are adopted 'voluntarily'; that 'free causality' is at the basis of all deeds arising from the individual 'power of choice'; and that such deeds deserve punishment (pp. 126–7).

We are still confronted by a 'difficulty': that of reconciling freedom with the 'nature' of beings, who are part of the 'world of sense' (p. 127). But, is there not a greater difficulty?: that of holding that existence subject to '**time and space**' is the 'existence of things in themselves' (p. 127). And, this confirms our view that time is a 'mere **form of sensible intuition**', which we have as members of the world of sense; so, the problem we need to solve is reconciling this conclusion with 'freedom' (p. 127). However, there is a further problem. Even if a rational being is free in relation to a particular action, despite being subject to the natural necessity of the world of sense, if one also assumes that God is the cause of the world, one seems to admit that the 'determining basis' of a human being's actions lies *'beyond his control'*, in a supreme being, upon whom his whole existence depends (pp. 127–8).

Well, if their actions in time were those of human beings as things in themselves, not appearances, there would be no 'freedom', and human beings would be **automatons** (albeit thinking ones), produced and operated by the **'supreme master of all artificial devices'** (p. 128). However, the problem dissolves, if, as we maintain, 'existence *in time*' is just the way that 'thinking beings' perceive the world (p. 130). Thus, as far as 'creation' is concerned, when we say that things in the world of sense are created, to that degree, they are *'noumena'*: for, just as it would be contradictory to ascribe the creation of appearances to God, so, too, it would be to describe him as the 'cause of the actions' in the world of sense, despite his being the cause of acting beings' existence as *noumena* in the world of understanding (p. 130). Therefore, we can hold that there is freedom, without impairing the 'natural mechanism of actions as appearances' for the fact that 'acting beings' are created relates not to their existence as 'appearances' but to their existence as *noumena* (p. 130). This could not be the case, if they existed 'as things in themselves *in time*', underlining the **importance of separating time (and space) from the existence of things in themselves**, as was done in the *Critique of Pure Reason* (p. 130).

*****

So, how can we reconcile the causality we experience in the world, to which human beings are subject, with the freedom of rational beings? We can do so by appreciating the distinction between the world of sense and the intelligible world, or world of understanding, to which human beings, as rational beings also belong. We have to understand that the very 'same action' which, in the world of sense, is 'mechanically necessary' can, as belonging to the 'causality' of an acting being in the 'intelligible world', also be regarded as 'free' (p. 132). 'Causality through freedom' must not be looked for in the world of sense, but in the 'intelligible' world (pp. 132–3).

And, there must be an 'objective principle of causality', which does not refer to anything else as a 'determining basis'; and this does not have to be 'searched for or invented': it is the '**principle of** *morality*', which is found in the 'reason of all human beings' (p. 133). So, the 'actuality' of the intelligible world is given to us '*determinately* in a practical respect', for the purposes of morality (p. 133). However, we cannot take this step with the second 'idea', that of a '*necessary being*', because to do so we would have to go outside ourselves (p. 133). It is our own 'reason' which knows itself, through the '**supreme and unconditioned practical law**', and so recognizes the being, who is aware of this moral law, that is 'our own person', as a member of the '**pure world of understanding**' (p. 134). Therefore, we can appreciate why it can only be '*the practical*' that helps us to move beyond the world of sense, and gives us knowledge of a '**suprasensible order and connection**': but only to the extent that such knowledge is needed for our 'pure practical aim' (p. 134).

Book II Dialectic of Pure Practical Reason (pp. 137–86)
Chapter I On a Dialectic of Pure Practical Reason as Such (pp. 137–40)

In both its '**speculative**' and 'practical' uses, 'pure reason' always has a '**dialectic**', for it seeks the '**absolute totality**' of

things, which can be discovered only in 'things in themselves' (p. 137). However, as human beings, we develop our 'concepts of things' from the information we receive through our senses; and, as this information is 'conditioned' by our senses, we know objects, not as they are in themselves, but only as **'appearances'** (p. 137). An inevitable 'illusion' arises: we regard the appearances of things as if 'they were things in themselves' (p. 137). And, indeed, we would not be aware of how 'deceptive' this is, were it not for the fact of our reason's conflict with itself, through its treating appearances, which are 'conditioned' (by our senses), as if they are 'unconditioned' (pp. 137–8). However, we are prompted to explore this illusion, in order to try to remove it; and this is 'beneficial', for it enables us to discover what we 'did not seek', but do require: **'an outlook into a higher, unchangeable order of things'** (p. 138). We are then in a position to 'pursue our existence in it', by following the **'highest vocation of reason'** (p. 138).

But, matters are still far from straightforward. The 'pure practical reason' seeks the basis for determining the will in our 'inclinations' and 'natural' needs, as well as in the **'moral law'** (p. 138). And, even when it has recognized that it is the latter that it seeks, it looks for the **'unconditioned totality of the *object* of pure practical reason'**, which it calls the **'highest good'** (p. 138).

One vitally important point must be emphasized about the 'dialectic' of **pure practical reason**, as it seeks to determine the concept of the highest good (p. 139). The pure will's only 'determining basis' is the 'moral law', and this is **'merely formal'**; it has no content (p. 140). Though **'universally legislative'**, it does not refer to any **'object' of human volition** (p. 140). So, although the 'highest good' is the pure practical reason's 'entire *object*', it cannot be the will's *'determining basis'*: that is the moral law itself (p. 140). And, indeed, great care is required here, for, if we put anything before the moral law as the determining basis of the will, and try to derive the '**supreme' moral principle** from that, it results in '**heteronomy**', which subverts morality (p. 140). However, if our concept of the highest good includes the moral law as its 'supreme condition', both the 'concept' itself, and the 'presentation' of the possibility of our attaining it, 'through our practical reason', become the '*determining basis* of the *pure will*' (p. 140). For then, in keeping with the '**principle of autonomy**' it is the moral law, and not anything else, which determines the will; and thus we avoid involving ourselves in any contradictions (p. 140).

Chapter II On a Dialectic of Pure Reason in Determining the Concept of the Highest Good (pp. 141–86)

There is an ambiguity in the 'concept of the *highest*', which can mean the 'supreme (*supremum*)' or the 'complete (*consummatum*)' (p. 141). That **virtue**, as '**worthiness to be happy**', is 'the *supreme* **good**' has been proved; but it is not the '**whole and complete good**' that '**rational finite beings**' have as the object of their desire (p. 141). This requires **happiness** as well. Thus, people receiving happiness, 'exactly in proportion' to their 'morality', is the '**complete good**' (p. 142). However, virtue is the supreme good, as there is nothing above it, whereas happiness, though 'always agreeable', is not, by itself, 'good absolutely' (p. 142). Now, in the highest good that we can realize through our will, virtue and happiness are thought of as '*necessarily* linked', but how are they linked (p. 142)?

The '**ancient Greek' philosophers** did not regard virtue and happiness as separate 'elements of the highest good', and sought to unite them (p. 142). However, whereas the

Epicureans regarded virtue as the awareness that following **morally prudent maxims** would produce happiness, the **Stoics** thought that awareness of (one's) virtue was happiness. So, for the Epicurean, the 'concept of virtue' was present in the **maxim**, by which the individual sought to promote his own happiness, while, for the Stoic, happiness was present in the 'consciousness' of his own virtue (p. 143). However, virtue and morality are 'entirely *different*' elements of the 'highest good', and they are connected **synthetically**, not **analytically**: one cannot say either that one who pursues happiness will find himself to be virtuous, or that one who pursues virtue will find himself to be happy, simply through this consciousness (p. 144). The connection is understood as an '*a priori*' and '**practically necessary**' one, which does not come from experience, as 'the highest good' is not based on 'empirical principles'; so, its '*deduction*' will be '*transcendental*' (p. 144). The '*highest good*' must be produced through '*freedom of the will*', so the 'condition for the possibility of this good must also rest solely on *a priori* bases' of (moral) knowledge (p. 144).

I *The Antinomy of Practical Reason (pp. 144–5)*

As the connection between virtue and happiness is not analytic, it must be synthetic: that of 'the cause with the effect', as it concerns a '**practical good**', which is 'possible through action' (pp. 144–5). So, either desire for happiness is the '**motivating cause**' of 'the maxim of virtue', or the latter is the 'efficient cause of happiness' (p. 145). The impossibility of the first relates to the fact that maxims which make 'longing for happiness' the 'determining basis' of the will are not 'moral'; but, the second seems impossible, too, because there is no evidence of a '**necessary connection**' between virtue and happiness, 'sufficient' to produce the 'highest good', in this world, however meticulously a person may obey 'moral laws' (p. 145). But, as the 'highest good' is an *'a priori* necessary object of our will' and is 'inseparably linked with the moral law', unless it is achievable, the moral law itself must be 'false' (p. 145).

II *Critical Annulment of the Antinomy of Practical Reason (pp. 145–52)*

The **'antinomy of pure speculative reason'** also produced a clash between 'natural necessity and freedom', but this was resolved by showing that it is not a 'true one', when the world and its events are viewed 'only as appearances' (p. 145). The very same 'acting being', when an *'appearance'* in the 'world of sense', is subject to its 'causality'; but (and in relation to the same event), insofar as that person also views himself as a *'noumenon'* in the world of understanding, whose existence is not determinable in time, he has a 'determining basis' which is not subject to 'any **natural law**' (pp. 145–6).

It is the same with the **'antinomy of pure practical reason'** (p. 146). It is absolutely false that pursuing happiness provides a basis for virtue. However, the proposition that virtue 'necessarily' leads to happiness is only false to the extent that this is thought of as a **'form of causality in the world of sense'**; and, if it is assumed that a 'rational being' has no form of existence other than this-worldly existence (p. 146). I am entitled to regard myself as a *'noumenon'* in the 'world of understanding', which means that it is possible that, through an **'intelligible originator of nature'**, the 'morality' of my attitude is necessarily connected with happiness (p. 146). However, if I were no more than a member of the world of sense, this could be no more than a **contingent connection**, which would not be enough for attainment of the highest good (p. 146).

The 'highest good' is, indeed, the 'highest purpose of a **morally determined will'**: the error lies in misunderstanding the nature of the '**universal law**' which connects 'morality' and 'happiness', and believing that there is a relation between things in themselves and appearances (p. 146).

Of course, it does seem 'strange' that both ancient and modern philosophers have convinced themselves that the connection, in a 'fitting proportion', between happiness and virtue, applies '*in this life*' (that is, in the 'world of sense') (pp. 146–7). Both *Epicurus* and the Stoics put the happiness that comes from awareness of 'virtue in life' above everything else (p. 147). In fact, Epicurus' doctrine tends to be misunderstood. He regarded the 'least self-interested performance of the good' as one of the greatest sources of 'joy', and differed from the Stoics (who did not make this mistake) only in assuming that those, to whom he wished to communicate the 'incentive to virtue', already had a '[virtuous] attitude' (p. 147). Now, of course, a virtuous human being, however much he prospers, will not discover joy in his life, unless he knows himself to be righteous. However, he cannot be made virtuous, in the first instance, by having the 'tranquillity of soul', which he will receive from such awareness, commended to him, because he has no idea of it (p. 148).

There is an '**error of subreption** (*vitium subreptionis*)' here (p. 148). A 'moral attitude' is 'necessarily' connected with the awareness of the will being 'determined directly' by the moral law; and the awareness that our 'power of desire' is being determined is invariably the basis for liking the resulting action (p. 148). But, it is not this 'pleasure' that determines the action; 'reason alone' determines the will, and gives rise

to the pleasure (p. 148). Being determined to action 'directly
by a pure law of reason' is '**sublime in human nature**', as is the
'illusion' (for such it is) of regarding the 'intellectual determin-
ability of the will' as an 'effect of a special sensible feeling' (p.
148). We must avoid 'degrading' what is the 'proper' incentive
to action, 'the law itself', and our respect for it, by confusing
them with 'feelings of special joys' (p. 149). We must ensure
that we do not act merely 'in conformity with duty', as a result
of the agreeable feelings we experience from doing so, but
'from duty' itself, which is the 'true purpose' of '**moral moulding**' (p. 149).

There is a more appropriate word than 'happiness' for de-
scribing the 'liking' we feel for our 'consciousness of virtue': it
is '*self-satisfaction*' (p. 149). 'Freedom', and being aware of one's
ability to obey the moral law, means '*independence from inclinations*' as 'motivating causes', which gives 'unchangeable',
intellectual satisfaction (p. 149). The 'inclinations' vary, and
strengthen when indulged, and so they are always '*burdensome*' to rational beings (p. 150). Further, although an inclination, like '**beneficence**', which inclines an individual towards
his 'duty', can make '*moral* maxims' more effective, it cannot
produce them; for to be moral, and not just legal, the moral
law must be the 'determining basis' of action (p. 150). Even
'sympathy' and 'compassion', if they precede 'deliberation'
about what one's duty is, and displace 'pure practical reason'
as its 'determining basis', lead to moral confusion (p. 150).

Through awareness of the 'power' of 'pure practical reason', and the resulting 'supremacy' over the inclinations,
which gives freedom from the 'dissatisfaction' that goes with
them, one experiences 'enjoyment' (pp. 150–1). This is not
'happiness', because no 'feeling' is involved; nor is it '*bliss*',
because one is not completely exempt from 'inclinations' (p.

151). However, to the extent that one is free of them, this enjoyment is 'analogous' to the **supreme being**'s '**self-sufficiency**' (p. 151).

By thus resolving the 'antinomy of practical pure reason', we can, in practical terms, regard a necessary connection between the awareness of morality and the 'expectation' of proportionate happiness 'as possible' (p. 151). However, we must recognize that pursuing happiness cannot lead to morality, so the latter is the '*supreme* good', and the 'primary condition of the highest good', while happiness is its 'second element' and a 'consequence' (albeit a 'necessary' one) of morality (p. 151). And, indeed, the highest good is only the 'entire object of pure practical reason', when there is this 'subordination' (p. 151). Reason commands us to regard attainment of the highest good as possible. However, we must also recognize that the necessary connection between morality and happiness is part of the '**suprasensible relation of things**', although its 'practical consequence', actions aimed at realizing the highest good, 'do belong to the world of sense' (p. 151).

III On the Primacy of Pure Practical Reason in its Linkage with Speculative Reason (pp. 152–5)

By 'primacy' among things 'linked by reason', I mean the 'preeminence' of one (p. 152). Now, if 'practical reason' can do no more than work on what '*speculative* reason' gives it, the latter has 'primacy' (p. 153). However, if practical reason has its own 'original *a priori* principles', with which particular 'theoretical positions' are connected, but into which speculative reason can obtain no 'insight', is speculative reason bound to accept these propositions (p. 153)? Or can it reject them, on the grounds that, although they do not contradict 'theoretical reason', their 'objective reality' cannot be authenticated through experience, putting them outside the boundaries that speculative reason has set for itself (p. 153)?

If practical reason was simply pandering to the inclinations, by putting forward pursuit of happiness as a moral principle, as is the case with '***Mohammed's* paradise**' or the teaching about '**fusion with the deity**', promulgated by **theosophists** and **mystics**, speculative reason would be entitled to do so (p. 154). However, if, as is shown by its awareness of the moral law, 'pure reason' can be practical, it is the same reason that judges by '*a priori* principles', for both theoretical and practical purposes (p. 154). Thus, even if, for theoretical purposes, reason is unable to establish certain propositions affirmatively, once they belong '*inseparably*' to the pure reason's '*practical interest*', it must try to 'compare and connect them' with everything that lies in its 'power as speculative reason', provided they do not contradict reason (p. 154).

In the relationship between 'pure speculative' and 'pure practical' reason, the latter has '*primacy*', in relation to matters that are 'based *a priori* on reason' and '*necessary*' (p. 154). There has to be this 'subordination', otherwise reason would 'conflict' with itself: pure speculative reason would admit nothing from pure practical reason into its 'domain', and the latter would extend its 'boundaries' over everything (p. 154). But, one cannot demand that pure practical reason be 'subordinate' to 'speculative reason', because, in the final analysis, 'all interest' is practical, and even speculative reason is only 'complete' in its practical use (pp. 154–5).

IV *The Immortality of the Soul, as a Postulate of Pure Practical Reason (pp. 155–7)*

To achieve the 'highest good' is the 'necessary object' of a will determined by the moral law, but the highest good's 'supreme condition' is the will's being wholly adequate to the moral law (p. 155). However, this is *'holiness'* **of the will**, which is un-attainable by rational beings in the 'world of sense' (p. 155). Therefore, it can be found only in an infinite 'progression' to-wards such 'adequacy'; and the 'principles of pure practical reason' require us to make such progress the 'real object of our will' (p. 155). But, as this is only 'possible' on the presup-position of the *'existence* and personality' of the same rational being, **'immortality of the soul'** is linked 'inseparably' with the moral law, and must be regarded as a **'postulate** of pure practical reason': that is, a *'theoretical* proposition', which can-not be proved, but nonetheless 'holds *a priori* [and] uncondi-tionally' (p. 155).

For God, to whom 'time' is nothing, this progress, which, for us, is 'endless', is the 'whole of adequacy to the moral law'; and all that his creatures may hope for is a 'share' in the 'highest good', based on their progress from 'the worse to the morally better' (p. 156). A creature cannot expect ever to be 'fully adequate to God's will', either now, or in the future, but can only hope to be so in the **'infinity of his continuance'** (pp. 156–7).

V *The Existence of God, as a Postulate of Pure Practical Reason (pp. 157–67)*

The moral law posed the problem of how to accomplish the 'necessary completeness' of the 'first and foremost part of the highest good, **morality**', leading to the postulation of '*immortality*' (pp. 157–8). What about the other part: 'happiness', in proportion to virtue (p. 158)? We must presuppose a '**cause adequate to this effect**', and postulate the '*existence of God*' (p. 158). The moral law contains no basis for a 'necessary connection' between virtue and proportionate happiness, so a '**supreme cause**' of 'nature as a whole', who is distinct from it, and who contains the basis of this connection, must be postulated (pp. 158–9). This need is '*subjective*', not '*objective*': there is no 'duty' to presuppose **God**'s existence (p. 159). Again, there is no necessity to presuppose God's existence '*as a basis of all obligation as such*', for this is based solely on 'reason itself' (p. 159). We are talking here of 'pure *rational faith*', as reason, in both its 'theoretical' and 'practical' uses, is its source (p. 160).

This enables us to understand why the ancient Greek philosophers could not solve the 'problem of the practical possibility of the highest good': they regarded the human will's use of 'its freedom' as the only basis of this possibility, without any reference to God (p. 160). Of course, morality is independent of God, but it is not, in itself, all that is required for the 'possibility of this good' (p. 160). The '*Epicureans*' adopted a 'false' supreme moral principle, that of happiness, but then their expectations of the highest good were correspondingly low: the happiness that could be achieved through 'human prudence' (p. 160). The '*Stoics*', on the other hand, rightly selected virtue as the 'condition of the highest good', but, by treating it as achievable in this life, they greatly overrated human beings' 'moral ability', and left out the highest good's other constituent: happiness, which is the particular object of the 'human power of desire' (pp. 160–1).

Only **Christian doctrine**, in the '**kingdom of God**', provides a 'concept of the highest good' which meets the 'strictest demand' of practical reason (pp. 161–2). The moral law is '**holy**', and so requires '**holiness of morals**', but the 'moral perfection', attainable by human beings, can only be virtue: which shows *'respect'* for the moral law, but recognizes the human tendency to transgress it (p. 162). So, in relation to the 'holiness' that Christian teaching requires, all the moral law offers human beings is infinite progress towards it: but also the hope of that progress continuing *'ad infinitum'* (p. 162). An attitude which is *'fully* adequate' to the moral law has infinite worth, because rational beings' inadequacy to their 'duty' is the only limit to the happiness that a 'wise and all-powerful' God is able to distribute (pp. 162–3). Although the moral law offers no assurance of happiness, as the '**natural order**' contains no necessary link between it and complying with the moral law, 'Christian morality' represents the 'world', in which human beings are wholly obedient to the moral law, as a *'kingdom of God'*, where '**nature and morals' are harmonized** (p. 163).

In this world, rational beings are given moral holiness as a 'standard', but 'proportionate' happiness, or *'bliss'*, is presented to them as an 'object of hope', achievable only in '**eternity**' (p. 163). Christian morality is not heteronomous: it preserves the **autonomy** of the pure practical reason, by making 'cognition' of God and his will the basis, not of the moral law, which is to be obeyed from 'duty alone', but only of achieving the highest good, on condition of obeying it (p. 163). Thus, through the idea of the 'highest good', as the object of pure practical reason, the moral law leads to religion, that is, to **recognition of** *'all duties as divine commands'* (pp. 163–4). However, any element of 'fear or hope', as incentives for moral conduct, which would destroy the 'moral worth of actions', is excluded: human beings can only hope to attain the highest good by harmonizing their will with that of the world's '**holy and benign originator**' (p. 164). Although the highest good involves the 'exact' apportionment of the 'greatest happiness' to the highest degree of 'moral perfection', the 'determining basis' of the human will is not the quest for happiness, but the 'moral law', which also strictly defines the nature of happiness (p. 164). Morality is not about how to make ourselves happy, but about how to make ourselves *'worthy* of happiness' (pp. 164–5). It is only with religion that there is the *'hope* for happiness', such that the 'doctrine of morals' becomes the 'doctrine of happiness' (p. 165).

As to God's *'ultimate purpose'* in creating the world, it relates, not to rational beings' *'happiness'*, but *'the highest good'*, which involves their worthiness to be happy; and, indeed, it is impossible to conceive of the *'benignity'* of God, who is also wise, as it relates to rational beings' happiness, apart from the limiting condition of harmonization of their wills with his holy one (pp. 165–6). For, nothing 'glorifies God' more than the 'holy duty', which his law imposes on us, being 'supplemented' by his **crowning this 'beautiful order with commensurate happiness'** (p. 166). Human beings, like all rational beings, are purposes in themselves: and should not be used, even by God, 'merely as a means' (p. 167). For, human beings are the subjects of *'the moral law'*, and therefore of 'that which is holy in itself' (p. 167).

VI On the Postulates of Pure Practical Reason as Such (pp. 167–70)

The principle of morality is the point of departure for the three 'postulates' of immortality, freedom and God's existence (p. 167). Although they are necessary practical *'presuppositions'*, which do not increase theoretical knowledge, they resolve issues which, for the 'speculative reason', were problems, and they give 'objective reality' to its 'concepts', which it could not provide itself (p. 167). The first postulate derives from the practical necessity of human beings' existence being sufficiently long to fulfil the 'moral law'; the second from that of their being independent of the 'world of sense', and thus able to determine their will according to the law of the '**intelligible world**'; the third from that of there being one who is capable of making attainment of the highest good possible (p. 168).

But, is knowledge actually increased by 'pure practical reason' (p. 169)? Yes, but solely for *'a practical aim'*, for it does not enable us to know what the '**soul**', the 'intelligible world' or the 'supreme being' are 'in themselves' (p. 169). Thus (and it is the same with the other two postulates), freedom must be postulated through, and for the sake of, the moral law, but this does not tell us how such freedom is 'possible', or how we are to explain it 'theoretically' (pp. 169–70).

VII *How It is Possible to Think an Expansion of Pure Reason for a Practical Aim without Thereby also Expanding its Cognition as Speculative (pp. 170–9)*

To 'expand a pure cognition *practically*', the will must have an *'a priori'* aim, which is independent of 'theoretical principles': that is, a '**categorical imperative**', which determines the will; and, in this context, it is the *'highest good'* (p. 170). However, its possibility depends on postulating three concepts, 'freedom, immortality, and God', to which no '**intuition**' corresponds (p. 170). Thus, the pure reason's theoretical knowledge is increased, but only in the sense that concepts, which were previously just 'thinkable', are now **'assertorically** declared' to exist, because practical reason requires them; but, this knowledge cannot be used for speculative purposes (pp. 170–1). The situation is that they gain 'objective reality', through the **'apodeictic'** moral law, which requires them as 'necessary conditions' of our being able to make what 'this law' demands our *'object'*; but, we cannot signify how these concepts refer to an object (p. 171). However, 'theoretical' reason was forced to acknowledge that *'such objects'* exist, although it could not 'determine them more closely' (p. 171). Thus, although our knowledge of *'suprasensible objects'* has not been increased, reason 'as such' has been expanded, as the 'practical postulates' have been *'given objects'*, and there is knowledge of the 'suprasensible as such', in that reason has been forced to recognize that there are *'such objects'* (p. 171). 'Solely' through the 'pure practical ability', these ideas, instead of being merely *'transcendent'*, become the 'bases' for actualizing the pure practical reason's *'necessary object'*, the highest good (p. 172). However, as soon as reason has received this expansion, it will then, as 'speculative reason', purify them, so as to prevent their becoming a 'source' of either **'superstition'** or **'fanaticism'**, which impede the 'practical use of pure reason' (p. 172).

In order to think of an 'object', 'pure concepts of understanding', or **'categories'**, are required, and these 'concepts' relate only to reason's 'theoretical use': that is, they must be 'based on intuition', so that an 'object of possible experience' may be presented through them (p. 172). Here, however, we are not concerned with knowing these ideas' objects, but with their having objects. The 'pure practical reason' supplies this 'reality', theoretical reason's only role being to *'think'* the objects 'through categories' of the understanding (p. 173). And, the actuality of such an object is made certain by one the practical reason provides in the 'concept of the highest good', namely, the *'reality'* of the concepts needed for realizing the highest good (p. 173). However, this does not increase theoretical knowledge.

*****

If the ideas of 'God', an 'intelligible world' or 'kingdom of God' and 'immortality' are '**predicates**' that come from our 'nature', we must not allow ourselves to try to turn these 'pure ideas of reason' into objects of the senses ('**anthropomorphisms**'), or believe that we have attained knowledge of *'suprasensible* objects' (p. 173). For, our thinking about them relates to their 'practical use', and is confined to what we require for the 'possibility of thinking a moral law' (pp. 173–4). Thus, we have a 'cognition of God', but in a 'practical reference' only; we can form no concept of his '**properties**', and are unable to develop any *'theory* **of suprasensible beings**' (p. 174). Indeed, if we ask the *'natural theologians'* to enumerate God's properties, such as his 'understanding' or 'will', there will not be one which is more than a 'mere word', once every 'anthropomorphic' element has been stripped out (pp. 174–5). Yes, we require the 'ideas of God, freedom, and immortality' as conditions of the 'possibility' of the highest good, but this relates only to fulfilling the moral law, and does not increase our theoretical knowledge (p. 175).

We can now easily answer the question as to whether the *'concept of God'* belongs to *'physics'* and also '**metaphysics**', or only to *'morality'* (p. 175). Clearly, having recourse to God is not a 'physical explanation', while it is also an acknowledgement of having reached the 'end of one's philosophy', for it involves assuming something of which one 'otherwise has no concept' (p. 175). It is not possible to draw *'safe inferences'* from our 'acquaintance with *this* world' to the 'concept of God', or to prove that he exists (p. 175). To be able to propose that this world was possible only through God, we would need to be '**omniscient**', and to have **knowledge of 'all possible worlds**', so that we could compare them with ours (p. 176). On the other hand, **we cannot know, or prove, that God exists merely from 'concepts'** (p. 176). An '**existential proposition**' is 'synthetic', not analytic: it goes beyond the concept to that which is not 'thought' in it, and posits an object, *'outside the understanding'*, which corresponds to the 'concept *in the understanding*' (p. 176). We can, on the basis of its '**order, purposiveness, and magnitude**', infer that this world has a *'wise, benign'* and *'powerful'* originator, but, as our knowledge of it is limited, and we are unable to compare it with other possible ones, we cannot infer that he is omniscient, **omnibenevolent** and **omnipotent** (p. 176). It may seem 'reasonable' to ascribe every 'perfection' to the world's originator, but **this would not be an inference** (pp. 176–7). If we follow the 'empirical path' of physics, God stays as an imprecisely *'determined'* and inadequate concept, while we can achieve nothing through metaphysics (p. 177).

However, it is different with 'practical reason', for the highest good is possible only with a deity of the *'highest perfection'*, who must be *'omniscient'*, to penetrate to the 'innermost attitudes' that underlie our conduct; *'omnipotent'*, to apportion the 'appropriate consequences' to it; and also *'omnipresent'* and *'eternal'* (p. 177). Thus, while nothing can be achieved by speculative reason, the 'moral law' determines the concept of God as *'supreme being'*, so this concept and that of the postulates of the practical reason belong to 'morality' (p. 177).

The absence, in 'Greek philosophy', of a '**pure rational theology**', prior to **Anaxagoras**, is not due to the ancient philosophers' lack of speculative ability, for nothing is more obvious than to replace the 'indeterminate degrees of perfection' of a number of 'causes of the world' with one who possesses *'all perfection'* (pp. 177–8). However, they considered that the world's 'bad things' ruled out such a 'hypothesis' (p. 178). But, once they began serious philosophical investigation of 'moral objects', they found that there was a 'practical' need, which disclosed to them the 'concept of the original being' (p. 178).

*****

This brings home the necessity and value, for '**theology** and morality', of the *'**deduction** of the categories'*, undertaken in the *Critique of Pure Reason* (p. 178). For, only **if the categories are posited in the 'pure understanding'** can one be prevented from developing '**extravagant**' **suprasensible theories**, like **Plato**'s (p. 178). On the other hand, if one considers them to be 'acquired', the outcome is that, like Epicurus, we will limit them, even for practical purposes, to objects of the senses (p. 178). However, we were able to establish that the 'origin' of the categories is not 'empirical', but lies 'a priori in pure understanding'; and also that, as they refer to *'objects as such'*, they yield *'theoretical'* knowledge only when 'applied to *empirical* objects' (p. 179). We can now also see that, when applied to an 'object' that comes from 'pure practical reason', they make possible 'determinate thinking' about the *'suprasensible'*, although only to the extent that this is determined by a *'practical aim'* and its 'possibility' (p. 179).

VIII On Assent from a Need of Pure Reason (pp. 179–84)

While pure reason's 'speculative use' just results in *'hypotheses'*, its practical application results in *'postulates'* (p. 179). A need of 'pure *practical* reason' does not concern satisfying an 'investigating reason completely', but relates to the '*duty*' to make the highest good my will's 'object', so that I can 'further it'; but this requires its 'possibility', and also postulation of the 'conditions' (which speculative reason cannot prove) of 'God, freedom, and immortality', which are necessary for achieving it (pp. 179–80). Of course, our duty is grounded on the moral law, which is 'apodeictically certain' and 'independent' of these postulates, and our obligation to obey it does not need to be reinforced by 'theoretical' opinions about things' 'intrinsic character', the purpose of the 'world order', or its '**governor**' (p. 180). But, the '*attitude*' that is necessary for pursuing the highest good must presuppose its possibility, otherwise, 'striving' for it would be 'impossible practically' (p. 180). The above-mentioned postulates relate to the '*possibility* of the highest good', not as an optional 'aim', but as the pure rational will's 'practically necessary purpose': that of obeying an 'unremitting command of reason' (pp. 180–1). Thus, as everyone is obligated by the moral law, the 'righteous person' may indeed '*will*' that there is 'a God'; that he belongs to a 'pure world of understanding'; and that his 'duration' will be 'endless' (p. 181). We must not allow 'this faith' to be taken from us: here, we have the 'only [case]' where the individual's 'interest' should determine his judgement, without his having to heed 'subtle reasonings' (p. 181).

*****

It is important to guard against a serious 'misinterpretation' (p. 182). It almost sounds as if '**pure practical rational faith**' is commanded, but that would be absurd (p. 182). Of course, the moral law itself does command us, but the 'possibility' of the highest good does not need to be 'commanded'; and nobody would assert the impossibility of the 'worthiness' of rational beings to be happy, in proportion to their obedience of the moral law, or of their possessing such 'commensurate' happiness (p. 182).

It has been pointed out above that we do not expect to receive happiness in proportion to 'moral worth', through the ordinary 'course of nature', but only by presupposing a 'moral originator of the world' (p. 183). I have not yet acknowledged that this perceived impossibility is *'subjective'*, but it is: our reason is unable to accept that nature can allocate happiness to moral worth so precisely, as doing so involves 'events' that take place in accordance with 'such different laws' (p. 183). But, it is impossible to 'prove' that this allocation cannot occur through '**universal laws of nature**' (p. 183).

The 'practical reason' provides an 'objective basis' for the command to 'further the highest good', but reason cannot determine objectively whether we should think of it as being achievable through 'natural laws', or only through nature having a '**wise originator**' (p. 183). However, 'practical reason' demands our being able to conceive of the harmonization of the '**kingdom of nature**' with the '**kingdom of morals**' as an *'objectively* necessary' condition of the 'possibility' of the highest good (p. 184). How we do so is our 'choice', but it is one that 'pure practical reason' determines in favour of God (p. 184). The 'principle' by which we reach this decision may be subjective, but it is the 'means' of promoting what is *'objectively'* or 'practically' necessary: thus, it is a '***maxim* of assent for a moral aim**' (p. 184). So, though our *'pure practical rational faith'* is voluntary, our decision to believe in a 'wise originator of the world' promotes a 'commanded' moral aim, and fits in with reason's 'theoretical need' to do so (p. 184).

IX On the Wisely Commensurate Proportion of the Human Being's Cognitive Powers to His Practical Vocation *(pp. 184–6)*

If human beings' 'vocation' is to work towards the highest good, their 'cognitive powers' must be considered suitable for the task (pp. 184–5). On the other hand, *'speculative* reason' cannot solve the most serious 'problems' confronting it, so cannot attain this goal unaided (p. 185). In fact, nature's gift of the appropriate power for the task seems *'stepmotherly'* (p. 185).

But, what if nature had made us capable of the kind of 'insight' or 'illumination' that we wish to have, or sometimes think we do (p. 185)? Short of a complete transformation of our 'entire nature', our *'inclinations'* always push themselves to the fore, and insist on satisfying our demand for *'happiness'*; only afterwards does the moral law curb them, and impose a 'higher purpose' (p. 185). But, in place of the current 'conflict' between the 'moral attitude' and our inclinations, from which **'fortitude of soul'** develops, human beings could be constantly aware of the *'dreadful majesty'* of *'God* and *eternity'* (p. 185). Then, yes, we would obey the moral law, but it would not be with the right attitude, for this cannot be produced 'by any command' (p. 185). The moral law must not be obeyed out of 'fear', but 'from duty', without which actions, and therefore individuals, lack 'moral worth' (p. 186). Human beings would become mere 'figures' in a 'puppet show', who *'gesticulate'*, but lack *'life'* (p. 186).

Our actual situation is very 'different' (p. 186). Despite all the efforts of reason, our view of 'the future' is 'obscure and ambiguous', while the world's 'governor' only permits us to 'conjecture' that he exists, rather than allowing us to see it

65

clearly, or 'prove' it (p. 186). However, the moral law within us promises and threatens nothing, but insists on '**respect devoid of self-interest**', and only allows us glimpses of the 'kingdom of the suprasensible', when this respect predominates in our lives (p. 186). Only thus will a 'truly moral attitude' be created, and a rational being become 'worthy' of sharing in the highest good to a degree that is 'commensurate' with his 'moral worth' and not just with 'his actions' (p. 186). We can see from studying human nature that the '**inscrutable wisdom**' responsible for our existence is as much to be venerated for what it has withheld from us, as for what it has given us (p. 186).

Part II Doctrine of the Method of Pure Practical Reason (pp. 189–205)

This cannot refer to '*scientific* cognition' of 'pure **practical principles**': it concerns how its 'laws' can be communicated to the 'human mind', and can '*influence*' its maxims, so as to make 'objectively' practical reason '*subjectively*' so, too (p. 189). Maxims are 'properly moral', and possess 'moral worth', when the moral law, and 'compliance' with it, provide the 'incentives to action'; and, in fact (and this may seem surprising), these have a more powerful effect on people than such 'enticements' as 'gratification' or the prospect of 'happiness' (pp. 189–90). And, indeed, unless this were the case, the '**spirit of the law**', as distinct from its mere 'letter', would never be found in our actions, and we would appear to ourselves as 'worthless' and 'depraved' (p. 190).

Of course, 'preparatory guidance' is required to direct a '**brutified mind**' on to the path of the 'morally good'; but, once this has done its work, the 'pure moral motive' must be 'applied to the soul' (p. 190). And this motive, which enables the mind to be governed by 'unchangeable maxims', and the human being to experience 'dignity', bestows on the individual's mind an 'unexpected' power to break away from attachments in the world of sense, which seek to rule it, and to discover recompense for the sacrifice in an independent '**intelligible nature**' and 'greatness of soul' (pp. 190–1). Indeed, our minds' ability to be amenable to 'pure moral interest' is the sole 'incentive to the good' (p. 191). I shall now briefly set out how 'genuine moral attitudes' can be established and developed (p. 191).

A 'mixed' company, which includes non 'scholars', engages in 'arguing', as well as telling stories and jokes; and no argument captures people's interest more than one about the *'moral worth'* of actions, and the nature of a 'good or evil action' (pp. 191–2). Furthermore, these discussions reveal the character of the participants: for example, while some will defend the good name of 'deceased persons', others will search out 'accusations' with which to 'challenge that worth' (p. 192). However, while the latter, rather than trying to 'reason virtue away', may just be applying well-intentioned rigour in what they accept as genuinely moral, the former, in defending the 'purity' of human 'intention' and 'virtue', in the examples discussed, appear to be motivated by the concern that, if their presence is denied, virtue itself will be regarded as 'a mere **chimera**' (pp. 192–3).

'Educators of the youth' should make greater use of this willingness of reason to examine 'practical questions' minutely (p. 193). Having taught the moral law to their pupils, they should research 'ancient and modern' history for examples of the 'duties' that they have expounded being put into practice, and encourage their pupils to assess the moral value of the actions concerned (p. 193). This will not only help to develop their 'power of judgement'; more importantly, by giving them repeated opportunities to identify, and approve, 'good conduct', and to detect and condemn any 'deviation' from it, it will give them a solid 'foundation' for 'righteousness in the future way of life' (p. 193). What is vital is that moral educators base their programmes exclusively on 'duty', and the 'worth' that accrues to an individual when he knows he has not 'transgressed' it (pp. 193–4). What they must not do is to commend the 'unattainable perfection', found in 'heroes of novels', which invariably leads to extravagant feelings, accompanied by neglect of common obligations (p. 194).

As to what is *pure* morality', well, only 'philosophers' can introduce doubt into 'this question', for '**common human reason**' has decided the matter by 'habitual use' (p. 194). We shall, therefore, illustrate the test of 'pure virtue' with an example that would be appropriate for the 'judgement' of a boy of ten, by telling the story of an 'upright' individual, whose acquaintances are trying to persuade him to take part in defaming an 'innocent', but 'powerless', person (pp. 194–5). They tempt him with the promise of 'gains', which he dismisses (p. 195). Then, they seek to intimidate him with threats: his 'friends' with loss of friendship; his 'relatives' with disinheritance; the 'powerful' with injury; and his ruler with imprisonment and death (p. 195). At the same time, his 'family', cowed and fearful, beg him to give in; but still he refuses to yield (p. 195). Would not young listeners to this narrative progress from 'approval to admiration', and, ultimately, to 'veneration' for one whose virtue is worth so much, not for its rewards, but its cost (p. 195)? In this example, the absence of any incentive related to 'happiness' reveals the 'purity' of the moral principle; and this shows that, for the moral law, and its attendant 'holiness and virtue', to have any impact 'on our soul', it must be applied to one that is unsullied with 'intentions', aimed at personal 'well-being' (pp. 195–6). The presence of incentives that concern individual happiness hinder the 'moral law' from influencing the 'human heart'; it is 'duty' that has the 'most penetrating influence on the mind' (p. 196). Today, we seem to think that what works best is to cultivate 'tender, soft-hearted feelings', but the inculcation of 'dry and earnest' duty is more effective in ensuring the 'progress' of imperfect human beings towards the good (p. 196). Certainly, engendering 'enthusiasm' for what is 'noble' or '**magnanimous**' in children is counter-productive, for their judgement is undeveloped, and it only produces '**fantasists**' (pp. 196–7).

What is essential is that '*principles*' are based on 'concepts'; otherwise, there is no 'moral worth', or awareness of a 'moral attitude', so the 'highest good in a human being' can never be achieved (p. 197). And, for these concepts to become 'subjectively practical' for the individual, 'self-denial' is required (p. 197). He must enter a 'higher element', where only exertion and constant anxiety about backsliding will enable him to remain: the moral law requires conformity out of 'duty', not '**predilection**' (p. 197).

What does it mean to act out of duty? It could be to lay down one's life in defence of one's country. Such an action is 'noble' and 'magnanimous', but some 'scruple' remains as to whether it is 'perfectly a duty' to do so on one's own initiative, without being 'ordered' to it (pp. 197–8). What is required is an '**irremissible** duty', non-fulfilment of which would be a breach of the moral law 'in itself', but which is performed at the expense of the most deep-seated and powerful inclinations, such that our souls would be 'strengthened' by witnessing the human triumph over everything that 'nature' brings into play as 'incentives' for not doing it (p. 198). The poet **Juvenal** provides the following example:

> Be a good soldier, a good guardian, or an impartial judge;
> If ever you are summoned as a witness,
> In a dubious and uncertain case, though **Phalaris** himself
>   should command you to be deceitful, and, having
>   brought his bull, should dictate perjury,
> Count it the highest crime to prefer life to honour and
>   to lose, for the sake of living, all that makes life worth
>   living. (pp. 198–9)

If an action involves a 'flattering' element, relating to its 'meritorious' nature, it is tainted with a degree of self-love (p. 199). But, to subordinate everything to the 'holiness of duty alone', knowing that one '*can*' do it, as our reason recognizes that we '*ought*': that raises us completely 'above the world of sense' (p. 199). This is what we must do. First, we must turn judging, according to 'moral laws', into 'a habit'; then intensify it, by enquiring whether an action complies with the law 'objectively'; and also teach ourselves to distinguish the various duties present in an action (pp. 199–200). We must also ask whether an action is performed, subjectively, '*for the sake of the moral law*', and so, by being correct, not only 'as a deed', but also in its 'maxim', has 'moral worth as an attitude' (p. 200). And, eventually, through awareness of cultivating our reason, we will become 'fond' of that which enables us to experience an increase in 'our cognitive powers' (p. 200).

However, at the outset, this is merely rejoicing in our power of judging. While we recognize a 'form of beauty', when we think in accordance with moral laws, we are still not interested in the 'actions' themselves, and the 'morality' of them, as we do not seek to do them (pp. 200–1). The next stage is to highlight the will's 'purity', through examples of actions where a truly 'moral attitude' is displayed, in that they are performed from duty, and not as a result of 'inclinations' (p. 201). This makes the student aware of his '*freedom*' to renounce 'even true needs'; and, although this may be painful at first, he will find the 'liberation' from the 'dissatisfaction' in which his inclinations enmesh him a relief (p. 201). Let us take, as an example, a situation in which someone is the only person who knows he has done wrong. He can ignore the reservations he feels, and remain in the thrall of 'vanity' and 'self-interest'; but, if he complies with the 'law of duty', he can feel respect for himself in the awareness of his freedom (p. 202). And, once a person feels himself to be 'inferior' and 'reprehensible', if he does not do the right thing, a 'good moral attitude' can be inculcated (p. 202). This just indicates the 'most general maxims' of how to approach 'moral moulding and exercise': each duty would need to be dealt with separately (p. 202).

Conclusion (pp. 203–5)

There are two things that impart 'ever new and increasing admiration and reverence' to the mind: *'the starry sky above me and the moral law within me'* (p. 203). The first begins from my position in the 'external world of sense', and enlarges my 'connection' into 'worlds upon worlds and systems of systems'; the second begins from my 'invisible self', and displays me in a truly infinite world, but one which is perceptible to the 'understanding' alone, and in which I perceive myself, not in a 'merely contingent connection', but in a 'universal and necessary one' (p. 203). The first perception minimizes my 'importance', making me a 'mere dot in the universe'; however, the second raises 'my worth' infinitely, for the moral law discloses to me a 'life independent of animality', which 'proceeds to infinity' (p. 203).

But, we must take care: observation of the world begins with the 'most splendid spectacle' that people can behold, but ends in '**astrology**'; morals start with the 'noblest property' of human nature, but lead to 'fanaticism' or 'superstition' (p. 204). Thus, the reason should only embark upon these investigations after careful reflection; and then, as has been the case with enquiry into the nature of the world, a 'clear insight' can be obtained into the '**world structure**' (p. 204). We must follow the same path when we enquire into our 'moral predispositions': this will lead to the '*doctrine of wisdom*', concerning not just what we 'ought *to do*', but also that which '*teachers*' should use for purposes of moral education (pp. 204–5). It is philosophy's task to pursue this 'science', and, although people in general do not need to do so, they must take an interest in the '*doctrines*' and the moral teaching it produces (p. 205).

Overview

The following section is a chapter-by-chapter bullet-point summary of the main points in the parts of Kant's *Critique of Practical Reason* summarized in the Detailed Summary above, and is designed for quick reference to it. Readers may find it particularly helpful for revision.

Part I Doctrine of the Elements of Pure Practical Reason
Book I Analytic of Pure Practical Reason
From Chapter III Critical Examination of the Analytic of Pure Practical Reason (pp. 114–35)

- Both practical and pure or theoretical/speculative reason are based on the same power of the mind, but operate in different ways.
- Pure theoretical reason starts with objects that are given to the understanding through the senses, and moves from these to concepts and principles.
- Practical reason is not concerned with knowledge of objects, but with the will, and it begins with the possibility that there are moral principles, discovered by the reason.
- It moves from them to objects, in order to categorize them as good or evil, in accordance with these moral principles.
- The supreme principle of morality does not come from any information we obtain through the senses, nor are rules of conduct based on inclinations.
- We understand that we can never be required to obey any moral law other than that of pure practical reason.
- The task of the analytic of pure practical reason is to distinguish the doctrine of happiness, which human beings are

naturally inclined to follow, from the doctrine of morals, which concerns the moral laws that we ought to follow.

- Examples can be used to illustrate the difference between the moral law, which comes from our reason, and rules of conduct based on inclinations.
- A generally honest man, tempted to lie for his own short-term advantage, is able to recognize the worthlessness of doing so.
- His practical reason judges what he ought to do, and combines with his self-respect to tell him he ought to be truthful.
- Pure practical reason does not repudiate our desire for happiness, but tells us that it must not guide us where our moral duty is concerned.
- However, it can be our duty to pursue our own happiness, including such sources of it as skill, health or wealth, as they may help us to perform our duty, while the unhappiness of poverty, for example, may distract us from doing so.
- But, pursuit of happiness is not a direct duty, and is not part of the supreme moral principle.
- We should be able to see, not just the possibility, but the necessity, of rational beings' supreme moral law deriving from the reason, for we ascribe freedom of the will to them.
- And this freedom, which must be assumed, because it is not achievable in the world of sense, is simply the will's independence of anything other than the moral law.
- However, our moral freedom is widely misunderstood.
- Causality, as natural necessity, has to do with things as appearances, subject to time, and is not the causality of freedom, which concerns things in themselves.
- If these two causalities were the same, none of a rational

being's actions would ever be under his control, but would be subject to the necessity of natural causes, so there would be no moral freedom.

- Therefore, the same being is subject to natural necessity, as an appearance, but is free as a thing in itself.
- For example, if a thief performed his action, according to natural necessity, he could not not do it.
- We are only able to say that he was capable of not doing it, because the moral law declares that he ought not to have done it.
- We must also reject a comparative concept of freedom, such as that offered by soft determinism.
- If we maintain that an action is free, provided it originates from our desires, this is like saying the movement of a clock's hands are free.
- If our actions are determined by a previous state, it makes no difference whether or not they are determined internally.
- They are still determined by natural necessity, ruling out genuine moral freedom.
- For freedom which is not absolute, is like that of a turnspit, which, once wound up, performs its motions on its own.
- However, as well as being subject to the conditions of time, the individual also thinks of himself as not subject to them, and as determining his behaviour solely by moral laws which he gives to himself through his reason.
- Thus, he is able to maintain his independence of the world of sense, and is capable of not performing actions which contravene the moral law.
- This is confirmed by our conscience, for, however cleverly we argue for the inevitability of our unlawful behaviour, we know that, by means of this freedom, we are capable of not doing it.

- We condemn the conduct, even of those who show every characteristic of unalterable criminality, as we believe that they have adopted their evil principles voluntarily, have the power of choice, and deserve punishment.
- It seems difficult to reconcile this absolute freedom with the fact that human beings are part of the world of sense, but a still greater difficulty would be to hold that their existence as beings subject to time and space is the whole story.
- But then we have a further problem: even if rational beings are free in relation to a particular action, belief in God as creator seems to place the origin of human actions outside their control.
- Well, if their actions in time were those of human beings as things in themselves, there would be no freedom, and they would be (thinking) puppets, made and worked by the supreme master.
- But, the problem dissolves, if existence in time is just the way that we see the world.
- For, just as it would be contradictory to ascribe the creation of appearances to God, so, too, it would be to describe him as the cause of actions in the world of sense, despite his being the cause of our existence as things in themselves.
- The fact that we are created relates not to our existence as appearances, but as things in themselves, underlining the importance of separating time (and space) from the existence of things in themselves.
- We reconcile the causality we experience in the world, to which we are subject, with the freedom we have as rational beings, by appreciating the distinction between the world of sense and world of understanding, to which we belong as rational beings.

- What is mechanically necessary in the world of sense can also be regarded as belonging to the causality of rational beings in the world of understanding, and so free.
- There is an objective principle of causality, which is not determined by anything else, the principle of morality, and this is found in the reason of all human beings.
- Our own reason comes to know itself, through this moral law, and recognizes the being who is aware of this moral law, that is our own person, as a member of the world of understanding.
- Thus, it is the practical reason which enables us to move beyond the world of sense, and gives us knowledge of a suprasensible order, but only to the extent that this is required for morality.

Book II Dialectic of Pure Practical Reason (pp. 137–86)
Chapter I On a Dialectic of Pure Practical Reason as Such (pp. 137–40)

- In both its speculative and practical functions, pure reason always seeks to get to the root of things, but this can only be discovered in things in themselves.
- As human beings, we get our ideas of things from the information we receive through our senses, so our knowledge of objects is as appearances, not as they are in themselves.
- As a result, we suffer from the illusion of regarding the appearances of things as if they are things in themselves.
- However, our urge to explore this illusion, in order to try to remove it, is beneficial, as it enables us to gain an insight into a higher, unchangeable order of things.
- Pure practical reason seeks to identify the highest good for human beings.

- But, there is the complication that it seeks the basis for determining the will in our inclinations and natural needs, as well as in the moral law.
- Now, the only proper basis for determining what we ought to do is the moral law, but this, though universally legislative, is formal, has no content and does not relate to any human wish or desire.
- This means that, although the highest good is the whole object of the pure practical reason, it cannot be the determining basis of the will, as this is just the moral law itself.
- Indeed, we must be very careful, for, if we substitute anything for the moral law as the determining basis of the will, and then try to derive the supreme principle of morality from it, this results in heteronomy, which subverts morality.
- However, if we include the moral law in our idea of the highest good, as its supreme condition, both the idea itself, and the possibility of attaining it, through our practical reason, become the will's determining basis.
- For, in keeping with the principle of autonomy, it is the moral law alone which should determine the will.

Chapter II On a Dialectic of Pure Reason in Determining the Concept of the Highest Good (pp. 141–86)

- There is an ambiguity in the concept of the highest good, which can mean the supreme good or the complete good.
- Virtue, worthiness to be happy, is the supreme good, but it is not the complete good for rational beings.
- In the highest good that human beings can realize through

their will, virtue and happiness are thought of as linked necessarily.

- Although it is hard to see how they are connected, the complete good requires happiness, exactly in proportion to how moral people have been.

I The Antinomy of Practical Reason (pp. 144–5)

- The connection between virtue and happiness is synthetic, not analytic.
- So, either desire for happiness is the motivating cause of virtue, or virtue is the cause of happiness.
- The first is impossible, because rules of conduct, which make longing for happiness the determining basis of the will, are not moral.
- However, the second seems impossible, as there is no evidence of a necessary connection between virtue and happiness in this world, sufficient to produce the highest good, however carefully a person obeys moral laws.

II Critical Annulment of the Antinomy of Practical Reason (pp. 145–52)

- The antinomy of pure reason, the clash between natural necessity and freedom, was resolved by showing that we need to distinguish between the world of understanding and the world of sense.
- When the world and its events are viewed only as appearances, we can see that human beings, as appearances in the world of sense, are subject to natural causality, but, as *noumena*, in the world of understanding, they are free and not subject to any natural law.

- It is the same with the antinomy of pure practical reason.
- Although pursuit of happiness is not a basis for behaving morally, the idea that virtue necessarily leads to happiness is only false if it is thought of as a form of causality in the world of sense, and, if it is assumed that rational beings only have this-worldly existence.
- When we regard ourselves as *noumena*, in the world of understanding, we can see the possibility that, through the creator of the world, there may be a necessary connection between morality and happiness, sufficient for attainment of the highest good.
- The highest good, bringing together moral conduct and happiness, is the highest purpose for a will which is governed by morality, but it is an error to think that there is a necessary connection between them in the world of sense.
- Two things are easily confused: the necessary connection between a moral attitude and awareness that our will is directly determined by the moral law, and the fact that when we are conscious of the latter, we are invariably pleased with the resulting action.
- However, it is reason alone, not pleasure, which determines the will, and gives rise to the pleasure.
- We must not degrade the proper incentive to action, the moral law itself, by confusing it with pleasant feelings.
- Further, we must make sure that we do not carry out our duty, merely for the agreeable feelings we experience from doing so, but from duty itself.
- In fact, 'self-satisfaction' is a better word than 'happiness' to describe our liking for consciousness of virtue.
- Being free and aware of being able to obey the moral law makes us independent of our inclinations as motivating causes, giving us profound intellectual satisfaction.

- Our inclinations, which vary in strength, according to how far they are indulged, are a constant trial to rational beings.
- Further, although an inclination, like active kindness, can incline an individual to do his duty, and make moral maxims more effective, it cannot produce them.
- To be moral, the moral law must be the determining basis of our actions.
- Even sympathy and compassion, if they come before deliberation about duty, and displace pure practical reason as its determining basis, can cause moral confusion.
- Resolving the antinomy of pure practical reason enables us to consider a necessary connection between morality and happiness as possible.
- However, happiness cannot lead to morality, so the latter is the supreme good, and the primary condition of the highest good, while happiness is its second element and a (necessary) consequence of morality.
- Reason requires us to regard attainment of the highest good as possible, but also to view the necessary connection between morality and happiness as part of the suprasensible relation of things.
- However, the practical consequences of this relation, actions aimed at realizing the highest good, do belong to the world of sense.

III On the Primacy of Pure Practical Reason in its Linkage with Speculative Reason (pp. 152–5)

- If practical reason can only work on what speculative reason gives it, the latter has primacy.
- However, what if the former has its own original *a priori*

principles, with which particular theoretical positions are connected, but into which the latter has no insight?

- Is speculative reason bound to accept practical reason's propositions, or can it reject them, as they cannot be authenticated through experience, which puts them outside the boundaries of speculative reason, even though they do not contradict it?
- If practical reason was simply pandering to the inclinations, by putting forward pursuit of happiness as a moral principle, it would be right for speculative reason to do so.
- However, this is not the case, and we are talking about two uses of the same reason.
- Thus, even if reason is unable to establish certain propositions theoretically, once they are an inseparable part of pure reason's practical activity, it must try to link them up with all it can establish theoretically, as long as they do not contradict reason.
- In the relationship between speculative and practical reason, the latter has primacy in *a priori* matters, which is essential, to prevent a conflict within reason.
- Without this subordination, speculative reason would accept nothing from practical reason, and would extend its boundaries over everything.
- We cannot insist that practical reason be generally subordinate to speculative reason.

IV The Immortality of the Soul, as a Postulate of Pure Practical Reason (pp. 155–7)

- Achieving the highest good is the necessary object of a will determined by the moral law, but its supreme condition is the will's being wholly adequate to the moral law.

- This is holiness of the will, which rational beings cannot attain in the world of sense.
- Therefore, there must be infinite progress towards this adequacy.
- As this is only possible on the basis of the continuing existence of a rational being's personality, immortality of the soul is inseparably linked with the moral law, and must be regarded as a postulate of pure practical reason.
- The theoretical proposition that the soul is immortal cannot be proved, but holds *a priori* and unconditionally.
- What we may hope for is a share in the highest good, on the basis of our endless progress from the morally worse to the morally better.
- We cannot expect ever to be fully adequate to God's will, now or in the future, but can only hope to be so in the infinity of our continuing existence.

V *The Existence of God, as a Postulate of Pure Practical Reason (pp. 157–67)*

- The postulation of immortality solves the problem of how to achieve the necessary completeness of morality, the first and foremost part of the highest good.
- We now need to deal with the second part: ensuring happiness in proportion to virtue.
- There is no basis, in the moral law, for a necessary connection between virtue and proportionate happiness, leading to the postulation of a supreme cause of nature, capable of producing this effect: God.
- This is not to say that we have any duty to presuppose God's existence, or that God is necessary as a basis of moral obligation as such, which is based solely on reason itself.

- Yes, morality is independent of God, but it is not, in itself, all that is required for the possibility of the highest good.
- Only Christian teaching provides a concept of the highest good, which meets the strictest demands of practical reason.
- It shows respect for the moral law, but recognizes human beings' tendency to transgress it.
- In relation to the holiness of morals that Christian teaching requires, all the moral law offers human beings is infinite progress towards it, together with the hope of that progress continuing indefinitely.
- An attitude, which is fully adequate to the moral law, has infinite worth, because their being unequal to their duty is the only limit on the happiness that a wise and all-powerful God is able to distribute to rational beings.
- The moral law itself offers no assurance of happiness, as there is no necessary link, in the natural order, between it and obeying the moral law.
- However, Christian morality portrays human beings' total obedience to the moral law as a kingdom of God, in which nature and morals are harmonized.
- In this world, rational beings have moral holiness as a standard, but happiness in proportion to morality, which is bliss, is an object of hope, attainable only in eternity.
- Christian morality makes knowledge of God and his will the basis, not of the moral law, which is to be obeyed solely from duty, but only of achieving the highest good, through obeying it.
- Therefore, Christian morality is not heteronomous, as it preserves the autonomy of pure practical reason.
- Through the idea of the highest good, as the object of pure

practical reason, the moral law leads to religion: that is, recognizing all duties as divine commands.

- But, Christian morality does not present fear or hope as incentives for moral conduct, as this would destroy the moral worth of actions.
- Human beings can only hope to attain the highest good by harmonizing their will with God's.
- Although the highest good involves exactly apportioning the greatest happiness to the highest level of moral perfection, morality itself is not about how to make ourselves happy, but about how to make ourselves worthy of it.
- Only religion offers the hope of happiness, making the doctrine of morals also the doctrine of happiness.
- God's ultimate purpose in creating the world does not relate to rational beings' happiness, but the highest good, which involves their being worthy of happiness.
- As God is also wise, it is impossible to think of his kindness, as it relates to rational beings' happiness, without its involving harmonization of their wills with his holy one.
- Nothing glorifies God more than the holy duty, which his law imposes on us, being completed by his giving us happiness in proportion to our fulfilment of it.
- Human beings, like all rational beings, are subjects of the moral law and ends in themselves, whom even God should not use merely as means.

VI On the Postulates of Pure Practical Reason as Such (pp. 167–70)

- Morality is the point of departure for the three postulates of the practical reason: immortality, freedom and God's existence.

- These necessary practical postulates do not increase theoretical knowledge, but they resolve issues which were problems for the speculative reason.
- Postulating immortality derives from the practical necessity of human beings' existence being sufficiently long to fulfil the moral law.
- Postulating freedom derives from the necessity for human beings to be independent of the world of sense, and to be able to determine their will according to the law of the world of understanding.
- Postulating God derives from the necessity of there being one who is capable of making attainment of the highest good possible.
- Thus, pure practical reason increases our knowledge, but only for practical purposes.
- This knowledge does not enable us to know what the soul, the world of understanding or God is in itself.
- So, freedom and the other two postulates are demanded through, and for the sake of, the moral law, but this does not explain the extent of freedom or its theoretical basis.

VII How It is Possible to Think an Expansion of Pure Reason for a Practical Aim without Thereby also Expanding its Cognition as Speculative (pp. 170–9)

- To expand knowledge in this way, the will must have an *a priori* aim, which determines the will and is independent of theoretical principles.
- This is the categorical imperative of the moral law, the possibility of which depends on postulating freedom, immortality, and God.

- The pure reason's theoretical knowledge is thus increased, but only in the sense that concepts, previously only thinkable, are now affirmed to exist, because practical reason requires them.
- However, this knowledge cannot be used for speculative purposes.
- The position is that the postulates gain objective reality, through their being necessary conditions of our ability to make what the moral law demands our object.
- Therefore, theoretical knowledge is compelled to acknowledge that they exist, although it cannot completely comprehend or explain them.
- So, while our knowledge of suprasensible objects has not been increased, reason as such has been expanded, in that it has been forced to recognize the postulates.
- Solely through practical reason, these ideas become the basis for realization of the pure practical reason's necessary object: the highest good.
- However, speculative reason then purifies these ideas, in order to stop them being a source of superstition or fanaticism, which would prevent their use for purposes of morality.
- We must not attempt to turn the ideas of God, a world of understanding and immortality, which are pure ideas of reason, into objects of the senses, or believe that we have attained knowledge of suprasensible objects.
- Thus, we are not able to understand God's nature or to develop a theory of suprasensible beings.
- Indeed, if we ask natural theologians to discuss God's characteristics, such as his understanding or will, they give us only words, once the anthropomorphic elements have been removed.

- We can now say whether the idea of God belongs to physics, metaphysics or morality.
- Reference to God is not a physical explanation, while it means we have reached the limits of philosophy, as it involves assuming something of which we have no concept.
- We cannot make an inference from what we know of this world to the idea of God, or to prove that he exists.
- To say with certainty that this world is possible only through God, would require omniscience and knowledge of all possible worlds, to compare them with this one.
- We cannot know, or prove, that God exists merely from concepts, for a proposition that something exists is synthetic, not analytic, and goes beyond the concept to that which is not thought in it.
- It posits an object, outside the understanding, which corresponds to the concept in the understanding.
- From the order, purposiveness and size of the world, we can infer that its cause is wise, kind and powerful.
- However, our knowledge being limited, we cannot infer that this cause is all-knowing, all-loving and all-powerful.
- If we stick to what we can know empirically (physics), God stays as an imprecisely determined concept, while nothing can be achieved through metaphysics.
- It is different with morality, for the highest good is possible only with a God who has every perfection.
- He must be omniscient, to penetrate to the innermost attitudes underlying our conduct; omnipotent, to apportion appropriate consequences to it; omnipresent and eternal.

VIII On Assent from a Need of Pure Reason (pp. 179–84)

- Our duty is to make the highest good the object of our will.
- This requires postulation of the conditions – God, freedom, and immortality – which speculative reason cannot prove, that are necessary for achieving it.
- Our duty is grounded on the moral law, which commands us, and which is independent of these postulates, and needs no reinforcement.
- However, the attitude necessary for pursuing the highest good must presuppose its possibility, otherwise striving for it would be impossible practically.
- So, as we are all under an obligation to obey the moral law, the righteous person may indeed will that he belongs to the world of understanding; that there is immortality; and that God exists.
- Nobody would assert the impossibility of rational beings' being worthy of happiness, in proportion to their obedience of the moral law, or of their ultimately being so.
- But, reason cannot accept that nature can make a precise allocation of happiness to moral worth, although it is impossible to prove that it cannot do so.
- Practical reason demands that we think of the harmonization of the kingdom of nature with the kingdom of morals as an objectively necessary condition of the possibility of the highest good.
- Although it is our choice how we do so, pure practical reason determines it in favour of God.
- While this decision may be subjective, it is the means of promoting the moral aim, which we are commanded to follow.

*IX On the Wisely Commensurate Proportion of the Human
Being's Cognitive Powers to His Practical Vocation (pp. 184–6)*

- If our vocation is to work towards the highest good, our cognitive powers must be equal to the task.
- But, theoretical reason cannot solve the most serious problems facing it, so cannot attain this goal unaided.
- Our inclinations force themselves forward, and insist on satisfying our desire for happiness, but the moral law curbs them and imposes a higher purpose.
- However, instead of the current conflict between a moral attitude and our inclinations, from which strength of soul develops, we could have been given complete knowledge of God's majesty and eternity.
- We would then obey the moral law, but it would not be with the right attitude: we would obey it from fear, not duty, so our actions would lack moral worth.
- However, the actual situation is that, despite every effort of reason, our view of the future is obscure and ambiguous, while God only allows us to conjecture that he exists.
- The moral law within us promises and threatens nothing, but insists that we respect moral conduct that is free of self-interest.
- It also gives us glimpses of the kingdom of the suprasensible, when respect for the moral law will predominate in our lives.
- This is the only route to a truly moral attitude, and for a rational being to become worthy of participation in the highest good to a degree commensurate with his moral worth.
- God is to be praised as much for what he has withheld from us, as for what he has shown us.

Part II Doctrine of the Method of Pure Practical Reason (pp. 189–205)

- Maxims are truly moral, and have moral worth, when the moral law, and compliance with it, provide the incentives to action.
- Surprisingly, these may affect people more powerfully than gratification or the prospect of happiness.
- Unless this were so, our actions would never reflect the spirit of the law, as opposed to its letter, and we would appear to ourselves to be worthless and depraved.
- Initial guidance is needed to direct a brutalized mind on to the path of what is morally good.
- This will enable the mind to be ruled by moral maxims, and give the individual the power to break away from attachments in the world of sense.
- The following is how genuine moral attitudes can be established and developed.
- Nothing is more likely to engage people's interest than discussion about the moral worth of actions, and the nature of a good or evil action; and this reveals the character of the participants.
- Educators should utilize reason's willingness to examine moral questions thoroughly.
- Having taught their pupils the moral law, they should research history for examples of the duties that they have expounded being put into practice, and encourage their pupils to assess the moral value of the actions concerned.
- This will develop pupils' power of judgement, and, by giving them the chance to identify, and approve, good conduct, and to detect and condemn any deviations, give them a solid foundation for righteousness in their future lives.

- A serious mistake is for educators to commend the unattainable perfection, found in the heroes of novels, which encourages extravagant feelings and neglect of duty.
- The nature of true morality is well illustrated by the following example which a ten-year-old child can understand.
- Every effort is made to persuade an upright individual to join in defaming an innocent but powerless person, but, despite threats and pleas, he refuses.
- Young listeners to this story would admire one whose virtue is worth so much, not for its rewards, but its cost.
- Here, the absence of any incentive, relating to happiness, highlights the purity of the moral principle.
- We tend to think that we should cultivate tender feelings, but inculcating dry and earnest duty is a more effective way of ensuring the progress of imperfect human beings towards the good.
- The moral law requires conformity from duty, not inclination.
- Acting out of duty could be sacrificing one's life for one's country, except that there may be some doubt as to whether it is definitely a duty to do so, unless ordered.
- We must bear in mind Juvenal's warning that it is the highest crime to prefer life to honour, and to lose, for the sake of living, all that makes life worth living.
- If an action involves a flattering element, relating to its meritorious nature, it is tainted with a degree of self-love.
- To subordinate everything to the holiness of duty alone, knowing that we can do it, as our reason recognizes that we ought, raises us completely above the world of sense.
- We must turn judging, according to the moral laws, into a habit.
- We must check whether an action is performed solely for

the sake of the moral law, not inclination, to ensure that it has moral worth, as well as being right.

- We must be aware of our freedom to renounce even true needs.
- Once a person feels himself to be inferior and reprehensible, if he does not do the right thing, a good moral attitude can be inculcated.

Conclusion (pp. 203–5)

- Two things fill the mind with admiration and reverence: the starry sky above and the moral law within.
- The first begins from our position in the external world of sense.
- The second begins from the invisible self.
- The first minimizes our importance, making us mere dots in the universe.
- The second raises our worth infinitely, for the moral law discloses the life of a rational being, which continues to infinity.

Glossary

A basis of all obligation as such. As the basis for morality/fulfilling moral duties. Morality is independent of God's will. See also Euthyphro dilemma below.

Absolute freedom of the will. See Freedom of the will below.

Absolute totality of things. The reason seeks a complete explanation of everything, which involves going beyond what can be known on the basis of sense experience.

Ad infinitum. Indefinitely.

An outlook into a higher, unchangeable order of things. See Suprasensible reality below.

Analytically/analytic. In relation to propositions, it means one where the predicate is included in the subject, or where denying the proposition would be self-contradictory: for example, 'This house is a building'.

Analytic (as of the pure practical reason). Analysis (of).

Anaxagoras. Greek philosopher and scientist, born in Ionia about 500 BC, who spent most of his life in Athens.

Ancient Greek philosophers. The philosophers of ancient Greece, in particular the Epicureans and Stoics (see below).

Anselm, Saint (1033–1109). Italian-born Benedictine monk, philosopher, theologian and author of the *Proslogion*, who was Abbot of Bec and Archbishop of Canterbury. See also Ontological argument below.

Anthropomorphism(s). Attributing human characteristics to beings or things which are not human. Here, Kant warns that our concepts of God (see below), an intelligible world (see below), kingdom of God (see below) and immortality (see below) are pure ideas of reason, and we must not think that we derive them from experience, or that our senses can tell us about suprasensible objects (see below).

95

Glossary

Antinomy of (pure) practical reason. The apparent contradiction (which Kant resolves) in the idea that the highest good involves a necessary connection between virtue and happiness. This could mean either that the desire for happiness is the motive for behaving morally, or that being moral causes happiness. The first interpretation is ruled out by the fact that it would involve obeying the moral law for an external motive, not for its own sake; but the second encounters the problem that, in this world, virtuous people do not always receive the happiness they deserve.

Antimony of pure speculative reason. The apparent contradiction (which Kant resolves) between the idea that human beings are free and therefore morally responsible, and the idea that they are subject to the necessity of natural laws, and therefore not free.

Apodeictic/apodictic. That which can be proved and is certain. A maxim (see below), based on interest or inclination, cannot serve as an apodictic moral rule.

Appearances. See *Phenomena* below.

A posteriori. That which comes after, or is based on, experience.

A priori. That which comes before experience, does not depend upon experience, and which holds true (or is claimed to) irrespective of experience. According to Kant, moral laws or principles are discovered *a priori* by the reason. So far from being based on experience of the world and human needs, they prescribe standards of conduct for human beings, irrespective of the human condition and general or particular human needs. Kant does not accept that all *a priori* propositions are also analytic: see Synthetic below.

A priori **categories/concepts of the understanding**. In the *Critique of Pure Reason*, Kant argues that we do not derive the general categories of thought, such as causality, existence, substance, reality and so on, which make thinking possible, from experience; rather, our minds impose them upon experience, thus determining the way that we think about the data we receive through the senses.

A priori **intuitions of space and time**. In the *Critique of Pure Reason*, Kant argues that we do not derive our concepts of space and time from sense experience, but impose them on experience, of which they are necessary conditions. He also refers to them as 'forms of sensibility': they shape our sense experience.

Aquinas, Saint Thomas (c. 1225–74). Italian-born Dominican friar, philosopher, theologian and author of the *Summa Theologica*, whose setting forth of Roman Catholic teaching was described as definitive by Pope Leo XIII in 1879. See also Cosmological argument below.

Glossary

Assertorically. Definitely, unambiguously.

Astrology. The practice of using the stars to predict the future.

Automaton(s). Robot or puppet: here one controlled by God.

Autonomy of morality. See Principle of autonomy below.

Autonomy of the will. See Freedom of the will below.

Beneficence. Doing good, being actively kind.

Bliss. Kant's term for the state of being in receipt of happiness proportionate to virtue.

Brutified mind. A mind which has become brutalized or animal-like, and not that of a rational being.

Categorical imperative. The imperative of morality, which commands unconditionally. What it commands must be done for its own sake, and because it is right, not in order to accomplish some further purpose, and so it may conflict with a person's inclinations. In his *Groundwork*, Kant gives five different formulations of the categorical imperative, including: 'Act only in accordance with that maxim through which you can at the same time will that it become a universal law'; and 'So act that you use humanity, whether in your own or in the person of another, always at the same time as an end, never merely as a means.'

Categories. See *A priori* categories of the understanding above.

Causality. Acting as a cause, the relation of cause and effect. Kant discusses causality in relation to moral responsibility. As part of the world of sense (see below), human beings, like everything else, are subject to the laws of nature, which suggests that they cannot be held responsible for their actions. However, as rational beings, they belong to the world of understanding, and are subject to moral laws, grounded on reason, which are independent of nature: thus, they are free and responsible for their actions.

Cause adequate to this effect. God, a being who is capable of producing the effect, and of apportioning happiness to virtue.

Chimera. Fantasy, illusion.

Christian doctrine. Christian teaching/principles.

Cognitive power. Power of the mind, ability to know things.

Common human reason. The reason/understanding of ordinary people, as opposed to that of philosophers.

Comparative concept of freedom. See Soft determinism below.

Complete good. People receiving happiness, exactly in proportion to how moral they have been: obedience of the moral law being rewarded with deserved happiness.

Congenital. Inborn, inherited.

Glossary

Conscience. Generally, human beings' awareness of what is right or wrong, which deters them from contemplating or performing certain actions. For Kant, it is reason judging itself, as to whether it has adequately scrutinized the rightness or wrongness of actions.

Consequentialist ethics. Ethical system which, unlike Kant's, decides whether an action is right or wrong on the basis of its consequences. See also Utilitarianism below.

Consummatum. Complete. See Complete good above.

Contingent connection. One that depends upon something else, and which might be other than it is.

Cosmological argument. One of the traditional arguments for the existence of God, which argues from the existence of the world and/or how it exists to God as its cause. In his *Summa Theologica*, Thomas Aquinas (see above) argues (second way or proof of God's existence) that, as everything has a cause, there must either be an infinite regress of causes or a first cause, and as there cannot be an infinite regress of causes, there must be a first cause of the world, God; and (third way or proof): the world consists of things that could not-exist (or 'contingent' things); but, if only such things existed, there must have been a time when nothing existed, in which case nothing would exist now; therefore, there must be a being that cannot not-exist (a being that exists necessarily). Kant rejects the cosmological argument on the grounds that it involves an illegitimate use of the principle of causality outside the world of sense (see below and *A priori* categories/concepts of the understanding above), and ultimately depends on being able to prove the existence of a necessary being (see below) and thus the ontological argument, which Kant has already refuted.

Critique of Pure Reason. Kant's major work on metaphysics. See Context section.

Crowning this beautiful order with commensurate happiness. Those who obey the moral law being rewarded with happiness in proportion to their worthiness of it.

Deduction. Justification.

Deduction of the categories. Justification of the view that the categories (see *A priori* categories of the understanding above) are not derived from experience, but originate from the reason, which thinks about and interprets experience by means of them.

Deontological ethics. Duty ethics; an ethical system, such as Kant's, which holds that we have a duty to perform or not to perform certain actions, because they are right or wrong in themselves, irrespective of their consequences. Thus, a deontological ethicist would say that it is always wrong to lie, even if, in a particular situation (for example, knowledge of the whereabouts of an escaped prisoner of conscience when asked), lying would produce more happiness (or cause less pain) than telling the truth. See also Consequentialist ethics above.

Design argument (for God's existence). One of the traditional arguments for the existence of God, which points to similarities between the world and objects designed by human beings, and argues that, as the effects are similar, the causes must also be similar. However, as David Hume (see below) points out in his *Dialogues Concerning Natural Religion*, any (relatively) stable environment, such as the world, which operates according to predictable natural laws, is bound to appear to be designed. However, there is no need to conclude that the world's stability must have been caused by God. A much simpler and more economical explanation is that the world is governed by an inherent principle of order. Further, such features of the world as diseases, hurricanes and floods indicate serious faults in the 'design' and the intelligence of the alleged designer. In the *Critique of Practical Reason*, Kant is sympathetic to the view that the apparent order, purposiveness and magnitude of the world (see below) support an inference to an intelligent being who designed it. However, he points out that this is not the same as an omniscient and omnipotent creator God. In the *Critique of Pure Reason*, he argues that it also involves an illegitimate use of the principle of causality and ultimately depends on the cosmological argument (see above).

Descartes, René (1596–1650). French philosopher and mathematician. In his *Meditations on First Philosophy* (Meditation V), Descartes puts forward a version of the ontological argument.

Determinable in time. Subject to time and part of the world of sense (see below).

Determining basis of maxims. That which decides the maxims, or rules of conduct, which we will adopt.

Determinism. The doctrine that every event has a cause, which, when applied to what are held to be voluntary human actions, suggests they are not actually free. Kant invokes the distinction between the world of sense and the world of understanding, to explain how human beings can be both absolutely free and morally responsible, yet subject to laws of nature. See also Causality above and Freedom of the will, Hard determinism and Soft determinism below.

Glossary

Dialectic. A debate or discussion. Here, within the reason, in its theoretical or practical uses, as it tries to resolve different philosophical issues. As Kant rejects intellectual intuition (see below), he does not believe in the possibility of Platonic dialectic, by which the mind gains access to an intelligible world/ultimate reality.

Doctrine of happiness. The doctrine (teaching, theory) that morality is concerned with the pursuit of happiness, or that happiness is the highest good. Kant (*Groundwork*) considers that people are strongly inclined to happiness, but that it is unattainable, because of the difficulty people have in deciding what would make them happy. They therefore pursue various inclinations, to try to achieve it, but these conflict with each other. Thus, Kant rejects any suggestion that morality is to be identified with happiness; that happiness is the end of morality; or that desire for happiness is a legitimate motive for behaving morally. However, as he explains in the *Critique of Practical Reason*, he believes that, although happiness is not the end of morality, the highest good involves human beings receiving happiness in proportion to virtue.

Doctrine of morals. The theory of morality, expounded by Kant in the *Groundwork* and the *Critique of Practical Reason*, that moral laws are discovered by the reason, and that such objectives as the pursuit of happiness are neither the objects of, nor the motives for, obeying the moral law.

Dreadful majesty. The magnificence/overwhelming power of God, which would inspire dread in human beings if they had definite theoretical knowledge of God's existence and attributes.

Edwards, Jonathan (1703–58). American Congregationalist minister, philosopher and theologian, who taught at Yale and was briefly President of the College of New Jersey (Princeton University). His books include *Freedom of the Will* (1754), *Original Sin* (1758) and *True Virtue* (1765).

Efficient cause. A cause which is capable of producing a particular effect.

Empirical. That which relates to, or is based on, experience. Empiricists maintain that experience is human beings' main or only source of knowledge.

Empirical elements. Essential components derived from the senses.

Empiricism. See Empirical above.

Epicureans. See Epicurus below.

Epicurus. (341–270 BC). Greek philosopher who settled and taught in Athens. He held that knowledge comes through the senses; that superstition should be eliminated; and that pleasure (as the only one known to the senses) is the sole good.

Error of subreption (*vitium subreptionis*). Error that occurs when something is obtained by misrepresentation or confusion.

Eternity. An everlasting/eternal afterlife, in which human beings will be able to attain holiness of morals (see below). Unlike traditional Christian teaching, which emphasizes being in God's presence/the vision of God, Kant sees eternal life exclusively in terms of the opportunity to achieve moral perfection.

Euthyphro dilemma. The question Plato poses, in his *Euthyphro*, as to whether something is right because God wills it, or whether God wills it because it is right.

Existential proposition. A proposition that somebody or something exists. The context here is the claim that God's existence can be proved from his essence, by means of the ontological argument, one of the traditional arguments for the existence of God. In the *Critique of Pure Reason*, Kant provides a detailed refutation of this argument. See Ontological argument below.

Extravagant suprasensible theories. Far-fetched theories about ultimate reality, of which, according to Kant, human beings cannot have any knowledge, as their experience is limited to the world of sense (see below). This is a reference to Plato's (see below) theory of forms. Plato held that individual things in the ordinary, visible world, which we experience through our senses, acquire their identity by being (in some way) copies of the unchanging forms or patterns of these things in an intelligible realm, to which our minds can give us access. Thus, something is round by being a copy of, or participating in, the form of roundness.

Fanaticism. Excessive (religious) enthusiasm, (religious) extremism.

Fantasist(s). Those who are subject to illusions. Kant is suggesting that, if moral education concentrates on developing enthusiasm for moral principles in children, they will fail to grasp the rational basis of morality.

Form of causality in the world of sense. See Natural necessity below.

Form of sensible intuition. See *A priori* intuitions of space and time above.

Fortitude of soul. Moral courage, which includes obeying the moral law for its own sake and not to avoid divine displeasure.

Freedom of the will. Although they are part of the world of sense (see below), and subject to laws of nature, human beings, as rational beings, are also part of the world of understanding (see below).

Glossary

Therefore, they are freely able to subject themselves to moral laws, discovered by their reason, and can be held responsible for their actions. Kant accepts that the existence of absolute human freedom (also called libertarianism) cannot be proved, but it is a crucial element in his moral philosophy, and he dismisses any attempts, through what he calls 'comparative concepts of freedom', to qualify it. See also Hard determinism and Soft determinism below.

Fusion with the deity. Being absorbed into, becoming part of, God or the universal spirit. See Theosophists and Mystics below.

God. Kant's concept of God is essentially Christian, but Kant interprets Christian teaching in the light of his moral philosophy.

Governor (of the world). God.

Happiness. See Doctrine of happiness above.

Hard determinism. The doctrine that the causal connection between human motives and actions rules out genuine human freedom. See also Freedom of the will above and Soft determinism below.

Heteronomy/heteronomous (of the will or morality). Heteronomy arises when the will is determined by considerations other than the precepts of the moral law, such as inclinations and desires, and is the source of spurious moral principles.

Hick, John Harwood (b. 1922). British philosopher/philosopher of religion and theologian, who was H. G. Wood Professor of Theology at the University of Birmingham and whose books include *Faith and Knowledge, Philosophy of Religion* and *Evil and the God of Love*.

Highest good. The *summum bonum* for rational beings, which is their obeying the moral law for its own sake and receiving happiness in proportion to the extent to which they have done so. See Complete good above and Supreme good below.

Highest vocation of reason. Working towards the highest good (see above).

Holiness of morals. See Holiness of the will below.

Holiness of the will. Moral perfection: a will that is completely adequate to the moral law, and which does not need to be commanded, in order to obey it.

Holy. That which is associated with, devoted to, set apart for, God or religion. Kant interprets holiness in terms of morality/the moral law.

Holy and benign originator. God.

Hume, David (1711–76). British empiricist philosopher and historian, whose works include *A Treatise of Human Nature, An Enquiry Concerning Human Understanding* and *Dialogues Concerning Natural Religion*.

Glossary

Hypothesis/hypotheses. A theory put forward as a basis for reasoning or a starting point for discussion.

If the categories are posited in the pure understanding. We apply the *a priori* categories of the understanding to sense experience, and this enables us to think about it. However, Kant rejects the view that the categories give us direct intellectual intuition (see below) of ultimate reality. See also Extravagant suprasensible theories above.

Immortality of the soul. The soul (the spiritual element within human beings) not dying, but living on for ever after the death of the physical body. Christianity brings together beliefs about immortality of the soul and resurrection, and teaches that the soul will be reunited with its body at the general resurrection. Kant's interest in immortality concerns its role in enabling human beings to achieve moral perfection in an indefinite existence after physical death.

Importance of separating time (and space) from the existence of things in themselves. In the *Critique of Pure Reason*, Kant maintains that we do not derive the concepts of space and time from experience (see *A priori* intuitions of space and time above). However, we tend to project space and time on to the things we are experiencing, and to believe that they are characteristics of things as they are in themselves, not just of the way we experience them.

Infinity of his continuance. Indefinite existence, as a result of being immortal.

Inscrutable wisdom. God's wisdom, which is beyond human understanding.

Intellectual intuition (faculty of). The view, held by Plato and other philosophers, that the mind can give us direct access to an intelligible world/ultimate reality. Kant rejects this view. Although the *a priori* categories of the understanding do not come from experience, they do not give us knowledge of the world of understanding/ suprasensible reality, which lies beyond experience. Believing that they do leads to what Kant calls 'extravagant suprasensible theories' (see above).

Intelligible nature. That which relates to reason and the world of understanding (see below).

Intelligible originator of nature. God, who is the cause of the world.

Intelligible world. See World of understanding below.

Intuition. Perception: the postulates of the practical reason (see below) do not correspond to anything we perceive in the world of sense (see below).

Irremissible. Unalterably binding.

Glossary

Juvenal (Decimus Junius Juvenalis: late first century/early second century AD). Roman poet and satirist and author of *The Satires*.

King Frederick William II of Prussia (1744–97). He succeeded his uncle, Frederick II (Frederick the Great), as King of Prussia in 1786. During his reign, religious and other forms of censorship were enforced in Prussia.

Kingdom of God. Jesus preached the coming of the kingdom of God, and the idea has been interpreted in different ways. In Matthew 6.33, he tells his followers to 'seek first his kingdom and his righteousness'. For Kant, the kingdom of God is bound up with morality: it is a world where human nature (the kingdom of nature) and the demands of morality (the kingdom of morals) are harmonized, and where human beings are wholly obedient to the moral law.

Kingdom of morals. See Kingdom of God above.

Kingdom of nature. See Kingdom of God above.

Knowledge of all possible worlds. Some philosophers, such as Leibniz (see below), have argued that this world is the best of all possible worlds, and that the only possible explanation of its existence and/or nature is that God created it. However, Kant argues that such a claim would only be justified if it were based on knowledge of all the possible worlds that could exist, which could then be compared with this one and a judgement made. However, human beings lack the necessary omniscience (see below), and so the claim is baseless.

Leibniz, Gottfried Wilhelm (1646–1716). German rationalist (see below) philosopher, whose writings include *Discourse of Metaphysics* and *Monadology*.

Libertarianism. Absolute freedom of the will (see above).

Magnanimous. Fair-minded and free of pettiness.

Maxim(s). A subjective principle or rule of conduct. The maxims human beings adopt must be measured against the categorical imperative (see above), to ensure their fitness to become universal laws, governing the conduct of all rational beings. Maxims must not be based on human needs or inclinations.

Maxim of assent for a moral aim. A principle which enables us to pursue a moral purpose.

Merely formal. The moral law does not have a content based on (satisfying) human inclinations. It is 'formal' in the sense that it prescribes the adoption of maxims (see above) that can be willed as universal laws, applying to all rational beings, not just to particular individuals. See also Categorical imperative above.

Glossary

Metaphysics. Study of what is after (beyond) physics, and which cannot be investigated by ordinary empirical methods; the investigation of what really exists, of ultimate reality. Kant rejects traditional metaphysics, because he believes that, as we impose the *a priori* intuitions of space and time (see above) on sense experience and think it through *a priori* categories of the understanding (see above), we have access only to things as they appear to us (*phenomena*), not to things as they are in themselves (*noumena*). However, although we cannot prove the existence of God, immortality and freedom theoretically, we know that they exist, because they are necessary postulates of morality. See also Intellectual intuition above.

Mohammed's (Mohammad) paradise. Kant contrasts receiving proportionate happiness, as a result of obeying the moral law for its own sake, with his interpretation of Islamic teaching about paradise, which he thinks panders to the inclinations, by putting forward pursuit of happiness as a moral principle.

Moral law(s). The *a priori* moral principles, discovered by the reason, which should govern the actions of all rational beings.

Moral moulding. Moral education.

Morality. See Supreme good below and Highest good above.

Morally determined will. A will that is determined by the precepts of the moral law and not by inclinations.

Morally prudent maxims. Subjective rules of conduct which are sensible, which promote the agent's happiness, and which may conform with duty, but which lack moral worth, because they are not performed from the right motive.

Motivating cause for the maxim of virtue. That which makes people behave morally.

Mystic. One who believes that it is possible to have direct knowledge of/contact with God.

Natural law. Law of nature, the causal laws operating in the world of sense (see below), to which human beings are subject as members of the world of sense.

Natural necessity. The operation of natural laws (see above) in the world of sense (see below).

Natural order. The predictable operation of natural laws (see above) in the world of sense, which make it a stable environment.

Natural theologian(s)/theology. Those who believe that God's existence and possibly attributes can be discovered/proved from experience and by the use of reason. Although Kant rejects the traditional arguments for God, such as the ontological and cosmological arguments (see below and above), he does show sympathy with the design argument (see above).

Nature and morals are harmonized. See Kingdom of God above.

Necessary being. God. According to Anselm's ontological argument for God's existence (*Proslogion*), God is a being than which a greater cannot be thought. Such a being (Anselm argues) must exist in reality (and therefore exist necessarily), because to exist in reality is greater than existing only in the understanding; so, if God does not exist, he is not that than which nothing greater can be thought, because a greater being (one that exists in reality) can be thought. Further, a being which cannot be thought of as not-existing is greater than a being which can be thought of as not-existing. But, if the being than which a greater cannot be thought can be thought of as not-existing, that being is not that than which a greater cannot be thought; and this is a contradiction. Aquinas (*Summa Theologica*) argues from the world, which contains generated and corrupted things that can not-be, to something that has necessary existence and cannot not-be: God. See also Ontological argument below and Cosmological argument above.

Necessary connection. A connection between things (such as virtue and happiness), which it would be self-contradictory to deny.

Necessitating conditions of past time. In the world of sense, past events cause present ones, present ones cause future ones, and so on; and nothing can escape this causal necessity.

Noumena(on). Things as they are in themselves, as opposed to things as they appear to us, because of the way we experience the world. Kant maintains that we experience the world in a particular way, and do not have knowledge of things as they are in themselves. See also World of understanding and World of sense below.

Object of human volition. Object(s) that human beings desire, human inclinations.

Omnibenevolent. All-loving.

Omnipotent. All-powerful.

Omniscient/omniscience. All-knowing.

Ontological argument (for God's existence). One of the traditional arguments for the existence of God, which argues from the concept of God to his (necessary) existence, as Anselm (see above) does in the *Proslogion*. The argument was rejected by Aquinas (see above) in the *Summa Theologica*, but revived by Descartes (see above) in his *Meditations on First Philosophy*. Kant provides a detailed refutation of the ontological argument (together with the other traditional arguments for God's existence) in the *Critique of Pure Reason*. He directs his fire particularly at Descartes' version, arguing that it confuses logical necessity and necessary existence. Kant's first point is that, if we build existence into our concept of God, denying his existence is self-contradictory, so, in this sense, he cannot be thought not to exist. But, this is to do with the way we have defined God, and does not prove that he actually exists. Kant's second point is that the ontological argument wrongly treats existence as an attribute or predicate, which it is not. To say, 'God is', adds no new attribute or predicate to the idea of God, but just affirms the existence of what is being thought, God, with all his predicates or attributes. If it did add something new, the idea would not correspond exactly to its object. Therefore, whatever the number of predicates, by which we think a thing, nothing is added to the concept of it by the statement that the thing exists. See also Necessary being above.

Order, purposiveness, and magnitude. See Design argument above.

Phalaris. Sixth-century BC tyrant of Acragas in Sicily, whose extremes of cruelty are supposed to have included roasting his victims alive, and whom it would be unwise to disobey.

*Phenomena(on).*Things as they appear to us, due to the way we experience the world, as opposed to things as they are in themselves. See also World of sense and World of understanding below.

Physico-theological argument. See Design argument above.

Physics. Study of the laws of nature, which operate in the world of sense. Kant's point is that God's existence and attributes cannot belong to the study of physics, because God is not part of the world of sense.

Plato (c. 429–347 BC). Greek philosopher, who was a student of Socrates and taught Aristotle at his Academy (the world's first university) in Athens. His writings include *The Republic*, *Theaetetus*, *Symposium*, *Phaedrus* and *Laws*. See Extravagant suprasensible theories above.

Postulate/postulate(s) of the practical reason. A necessary condition: in the *Critique of Practical Reason*, of morality and the possibility of attaining the highest good (see above). The three postulates are freedom (see Freedom of the will above), the immortality of the soul (see above and Soul below) and God (see above).

Practical freedom. See Freedom of the will above.

Practical good. A moral act.

Practical law(s). Moral law(s) (see above).

Practical principle(s). Moral law(s) (see above).

Glossary

Practical reason. Reason in its practical use, as it concerns morality, the moral law.

Practically necessary. Necessary for purposes of morality.

Predicate(s). The part of a statement/proposition in which something is said about the subject.

Predilection. Personal preference, inclination.

Principle of autonomy. The principle of the independence of morality/moral laws, which must be obeyed for their own sake and for no other reason.

Principle of morality. Moral law(s), which derive from the reason, and to which human beings, as rational beings, voluntarily subject themselves.

Properties (of God). God's characteristics or attributes, such as his omniscience and omnipotence (see above).

Pure intelligence. A rational being, a human being as part of the world of understanding (see above).

Pure practical law of reason. The moral law (see above).

Pure practical rational faith. Kant's moralized version of Christianity, which recognizes obedience to the moral law as the only service that God requires, and which treats moral duties as divine commands. Kant discusses his interpretation of Christianity and Christian doctrine at length in his *Religion Within the Boundaries of Mere Reason*.

Pure practical reason. See Practical reason above.

Pure rational theology. See Theology below.

Pure reason. Here, theoretical or speculative reason (see below).

Pure will. A will that is determined by the precepts of the moral law and not by desires and inclinations.

Pure world of understanding. See World of understanding below.

Rashdall, Hastings (1858–1924). British philosopher, fellow of New College, Oxford and author of *The Theory of Good and Evil*.

Rational being(s)/rational finite being(s). Any being possessing reason. Kant makes the point that the moral law would apply to any rational being, not just to human beings. In the *Groundwork*, Kant affirms that human and all rational beings have absolute worth, and must be treated 'always at the same time as an end, never merely as a means'. See also Categorical imperative above.

Rationalism/rationalist. The view of such philosophers as Descartes (see above) and Leibniz (see above) that reason, not (sense) experience, is the source of human knowledge. Although he rejects empiricism (see above), Kant is not an orthodox rationalist, holding that, although all knowledge begins with experience, it does not all arise from experience.

Recognition of all duties as divine commands. Although morality is independent of God's will, and the precepts of the moral law are to be obeyed for their own sake, they can also be regarded as divine commands.

Repentance. Feeling sorrow or regret for an act, particularly a sin (offence against God/divine law).

Respect devoid of self-interest. Obeying the moral law, without any hope of gaining benefits from doing so.

Ross, Sir William David (1877–1971). British philosopher, who was White's Professor of Moral Philosopher at the University of Oxford and later Provost of Oriel College and Vice-Chancellor. Author of *Aristotle*, *The Right and the Good* and *Foundations of Ethics*.

Self-satisfaction. The term Kant suggests for the pleasure we feel when conscious of our own virtue/that we obey the moral law for its own sake. However, the term has unfortunate connotations of self-satisfied self-righteousness.

Self-sufficiency. Being free, as God is, of the promptings of the inclinations, which Kant considers a trial to rational beings.

Sensibility. The senses; the data we receive through the senses.

Soft determinism. What Kant terms a 'comparative concept of freedom', which argues that human freedom is compatible with determinism (see above), and that human beings are free, unless subject to external coercion. This is the position David Hume (see above) adopts in his *Enquiry Concerning Human Understanding*.

Soul. In Christianity, the spiritual element within human beings, which is the seat of personality and individual identity, which lives on after death, and which will be reunited with its body at the general resurrection. For Kant, the idea of a permanent, immortal soul is an idea of pure reason. Its existence cannot be known or proved empirically or by the theoretical reason (see Intellectual intuition above), but it can be postulated (and to that extent known) by the practical reason, for the purpose of morality.

Speculative (reason). See Theoretical reason below.

Spirit of the law. This is being observed when rational beings are motivated to action by the precepts of the moral law, and not by hopes/fears about the benefits/penalties of doing or not doing so.

Steady chain of nature. The natural necessity (see above) of the laws of nature.

Stepmotherly. Mean, grudging.

Glossary

Stoics. School of Greek philosophy, which taught self-control and uncomplaining fortitude in the face of pain and adversity.

Sublime in human nature. What is impressive or awe-inspiring about human nature.

Superstition. Belief or practice not based on reason or experience.

Suprasensible objects/beings. See Suprasensible reality below.

Suprasensible order and connection. Order and relation of things which is beyond the world of sense (see below) and inaccessible to empirical observation.

Suprasensible reality. A world/reality that is beyond/transcends the ordinary physical world that we know about through experience/the senses.

Suprasensible relation of things. See Suprasensible order and connection above.

Supreme and unconditioned practical law. Moral law (see above).

Supreme being. God.

Supreme cause. God.

Supreme good. Being worthy of happiness, through having obeyed the moral law for its own sake.

Supreme master of all artificial devices. What God would be if he controlled/manipulated the actions of rational beings.

Supreme moral principle. The moral law, which must be obeyed for its own sake and not as the means to happiness.

Supreme practical principle. See Supreme moral principle above.

Supremum. Supreme. See Supreme good above.

Synthetically/synthetic. In relation to propositions, it means those where the predicate is not included in the subject, which cannot be verified by analysis of the concept(s) involved, and which therefore convey actual information. Most philosophers hold that synthetic propositions are also *a posteriori*, that is, derive the information they give from experience. However, Kant maintains that there are also *a priori* (see above) synthetic propositions, such as those of morality.

The starry sky above me and the moral law within me. The two things which fill the mind with admiration and reverence. While the first sight makes the individual human being seem insignificant, as a tiny part of the world of sense, contemplation of the second underlines his importance as a rational being, who belongs to the world of understanding and is capable of freely obeying the moral law.

Theology. Generally, setting out the beliefs and teachings of a religion in a systematic way; academic discipline concerned with the study of religion/religious beliefs. Kant also refers to a 'pure rational theology', which deals with God as a necessary postulate of the practical reason and morality.

Theory of forms. See Extravagant suprasensible theories above.

Theory of suprasensible beings. Metaphysical theories about God and/or ultimate reality, which go beyond the limits of human knowledge, and are therefore mere speculation. See also Metaphysics above.

Theosophists. Literally 'divine wisdom', and could refer to any direct knowledge of God. Modern theosophy is associated with the work of Helena Petrovna Blavatsky (1831–91) and Annie Besant (1847–1933), and teaches the animation of the universe by a single life force, reincarnation and evolution towards higher spiritual levels.

Things in themselves/thing in itself. See *Noumena* above.

This would not be an inference. We cannot infer, from the fact that the world is a stable environment, that its cause must be an all-knowing, all-loving and all-powerful God: the evidence is insufficient to support the conclusion. See also Design argument above.

Time and space. See *A priori* intuitions of space and time above.

Traditional arguments for the existence of God. See Cosmological, Design and Ontological arguments above.

Transcendent/transcendental. Non-empirical, that which is not associated with or derived from empirical experience/the world of the senses (see below).

Transcendent concept of freedom/transcendental freedom. Absolute freedom. See Freedom of the will above.

Ultimate purpose. God's reason(s) for creating the world and rational beings: their attainment of the highest good.

Unconditioned totality of the object of pure practical reason. The highest good (see above).

Universal law. Here, the universal law by which happiness is apportioned to morality.

Universal laws of nature. Laws of nature, which are universal in their operation, and determine everything that happens in the world of sense (see below). Kant acknowledges that there is no objective proof that virtue cannot be rewarded with the happiness it deserves by means of these laws.

Universally legislative. Binding on all rational beings in all circumstances.

Utilitarianism. Consequentialist ethical system, which holds that pleasure/happiness is the ultimate good and that actions are right to the extent that they maximize pleasure/happiness or minimize pain.

Virtue. Goodness, moral excellence: obeying the moral law for its own sake.

We cannot know, or prove, that God exists merely from concepts. This is what the ontological argument attempts to do. See Necessary being and Ontological argument above.

Whole and complete good. Those who obey the moral law for its own sake receiving the happiness they deserve.

Wise originator (of nature). God.

World of sense. The phenomenal world or world as it appears to us, due to the way that we, as human beings, experience it, and as part of which we are subject to the causal necessity of natural laws. See also *Phenomena* and *Noumena* above and World of understanding below.

World of understanding. As rational beings, human beings belong to the world of understanding or intellectual or noumenal world, as well as the world of sense or phenomenal world (see above). As part of the latter, they are subject to the causality of laws of nature, but, as part of the world of understanding, they are subject to laws which are independent of nature, and which are grounded in reason: thus, they are free to obey the moral law, a law to which they freely subject themselves. See also *Noumena*, *Phenomena* and World of sense above.

World structure. Kant is referring to his enquiries in the *Critique of Pure Reason*. See above.

Worthiness to be happy. The supreme good for rational beings is being worthy of happiness, as a result of having obeyed the moral law for its own sake; but this is not the complete good, which requires happiness as well.

Index

Index

Index